THE TAROT
SPELLCASTER

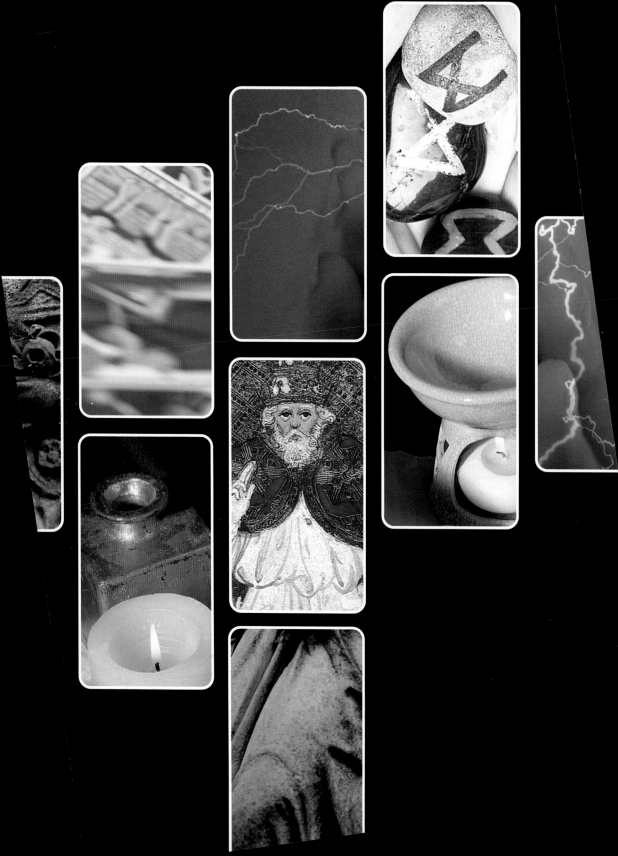

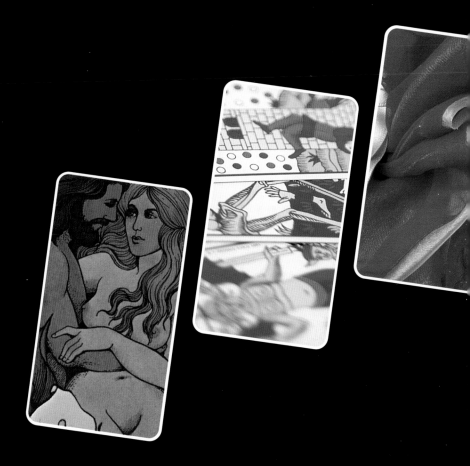

THE TAROT SPELLCASTER

Over 40 spells to enhance your life
with the power of tarot magic

Terry Donaldson

FAIR WINDS
PRESS
BRIGHTON, SUSSEX

A QUARTO BOOK

0 9 8 7 6 5 4 3 2 1

ISBN 1-931412-96-0

Fair Winds Press
33 Commercial Street
Gloucester, MA 01930
USA

Sheridan House
112–116A Western Road
Hove
East Sussex BN3 1DD
England

Copyright © 2001 Quarto Publishing plc

Conceived, designed, and produced by
Quarto Publishing plc
The Old Brewery
6 Blundell Street
London N7 9BH

QUAR· TARO

Senior editor: Michelle Pickering
Art editor: Jörn Kröger
Designer: Julie Francis
Photographer: Michael Wicks
Stylist: Lindsay Phillips
Illustrators: Ch'en-Ling, Sarah Young
Model: Natasha Davies
Indexer: Dorothy Frame

Art director: Moira Clinch
Publisher: Piers Spence

Manufactured by Regent Publishing Services Ltd,
Hong Kong
Printed by Leefung-Asco Printers Ltd, China

Warning
Burning candles and incense, and inscribing candles
using a knife or similar implement, can be hazardous.
The author, publisher, and copyright holder assume
no responsibility for any injury or damage caused or
sustained while casting any of the spells in this book.

Dedication
To Claire McKinyen, with love

INTRODUCTION

What is magic? What is a spell? Can we, living at the beginning of the 21st century with all our technological and scientific knowledge, really be expected to believe in such things, or are they just another form of escapism from the harshness of modern life?

There are many theories about why and how spells work. Some people believe that supernatural forces are involved, others that the unconscious mind is a powerful instrument that responds to symbols and ritualistic actions in a very special and interesting way. In other words, a spell is simply a way of concentrating the power of the mind in order to bring about a desired result. It allows you to take greater control, and thereby more responsibility, over your own life. It is not an escape from reality, but an embracing of it.

None of the spells in this book requires you to believe in anything that you have not personally experienced. Nor do you have to accept the existence of the supernatural. All you need to do is keep an open mind. There are spells for just about every aspect of life: career, love, friendship, self-development, and so on. The spells draw their inspiration primarily from the rich symbolism of the tarot, but also include elements from the Kabbalah, African systems of magic, astrology, angelic invocation,

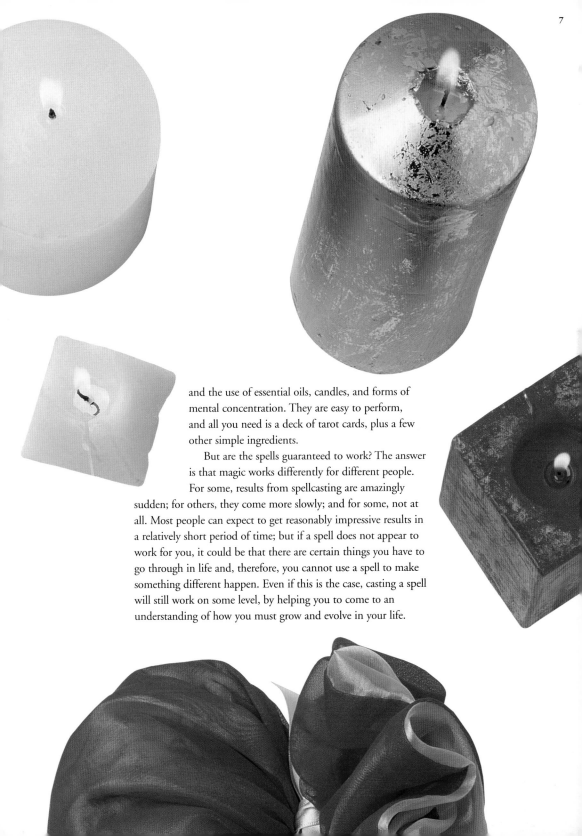

and the use of essential oils, candles, and forms of mental concentration. They are easy to perform, and all you need is a deck of tarot cards, plus a few other simple ingredients.

But are the spells guaranteed to work? The answer is that magic works differently for different people. For some, results from spellcasting are amazingly sudden; for others, they come more slowly; and for some, not at all. Most people can expect to get reasonably impressive results in a relatively short period of time; but if a spell does not appear to work for you, it could be that there are certain things you have to go through in life and, therefore, you cannot use a spell to make something different happen. Even if this is the case, casting a spell will still work on some level, by helping you to come to an understanding of how you must grow and evolve in your life.

The tarot, with its rich layers of symbolism, provides
the perfect focus for spellcasting. This chapter discusses
the tarot's mysterious origins, how magic works, and the
ethics of casting spells, then gives detailed guidance for
preparing yourself for spellcasting. This includes gathering
tools and ingredients, choosing and preparing tarot cards,
setting up an altar, and achieving a magical state of mind.
An easy-to-use spellfinder summarizes the intent of all the
spells in the book so that you can see at a glance which
spell to cast for your desired outcome.

tarot ✠ magic

The tarot consists of seventy-eight cards. The twenty-two major arcana or trump cards have titles and are numbered from one to twenty-one; the Fool is usually unnumbered or labeled zero. The fifty-six minor arcana cards comprise four suits: Cups, Wands, Coins, and Swords. Each suit has fourteen cards: ten pip cards, numbered ace to ten, and four court cards—page, knight, queen, and king.

THE HISTORY OF THE TAROT

The tarot first appeared in northern Italy during the latter half of the 14th century, but the origins of its imagery go back much farther than that. One theory is that tarot cards are all that remain from hieroglyphic books destroyed during the burning of the great library of Alexandria. Another theory is that the tarot was created by a group of scholars who met in Fez in Morocco around the year 1200 to establish a universal symbolic language. Others believe that gypsies brought the cards to Europe in the late 14th century, when they were forced to flee persecution in India.

One thing we know for sure is that, in 1392, Jacquemin Gringonneur was paid 56 *sols de Paris* (gold pieces) to paint three decks of tarot cards in gilt for King Charles VI of France. Another famous early deck is the 15th-century Italian Visconti-Sforza tarot (modern reproductions are pictured on the left). The most influential tarot imagery, however, is the medieval-inspired designs of the 18th-century Tarot de Marseille (some cards from this deck are pictured on page 12). The word tarot itself is a French adaptation of the Italian word *tarocco* or *tarocchi*, the name of a card game, and the word trump derives from the Italian *trionf*, meaning triumph (in the game, the major arcana trump cards triumph over the minor arcana).

TAROT AND THE KABBALAH

In the 19th century, Eliphas Lévi and Papus drew attention to the numerical similarities between the twenty-two major arcana cards, the twenty-two letters of the Hebrew alphabet, and the twenty-two pathways connecting the ten spheres in the tree of life of the Jewish Kabbalah. The pathways—each associated with a letter of the Hebrew alphabet—are linked with certain spiritual experiences that each of us must traverse in order to achieve higher states of awareness and understanding. Lévi, and Papus after him, developed the theory that the cards of the major arcana also symbolize this spiritual journey of mankind.

THE TREE OF LIFE

This diagram shows the Hebrew names of the ten spheres of the tree of life of the Kabbalah, their translation, and the minor arcana cards with which the spheres are associated. Each pathway is linked with a letter of the Hebrew alphabet and a card from the major arcana.

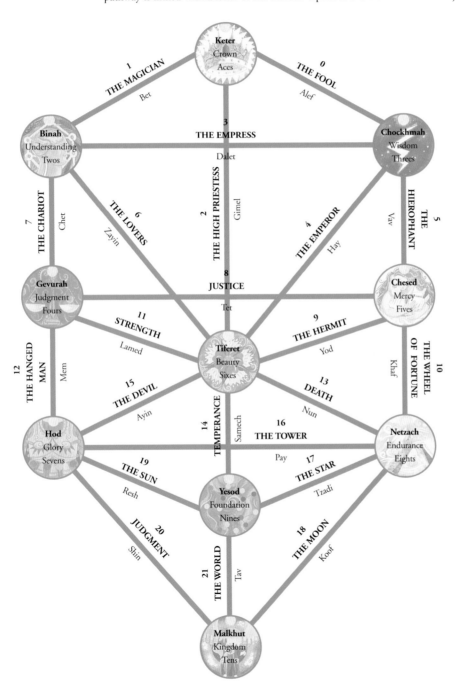

TAROT AND OCCULTISM

During the 19th and early 20th centuries, numerous mystical organizations, such as the Order of the Golden Dawn, Order of the Silver Star, and Order of the Temple of the East, sprang up, with the avowed purpose of training people in magical and esoteric techniques as a means of creating a spiritual dynamic capable of accelerating the evolution of humanity. These groups expanded the ideas of Lévi and Papus, and are largely responsible for the way in which we interpret tarot cards to this day.

Two popular tarot decks—the Thoth and the Rider-Waite—were designed by members of the Order of the Golden Dawn. This group of mystics is also largely responsible for the astrological associations of the tarot. Although these associations can vary to some degree, most commonly the major arcana is linked with the twelve signs of the zodiac and ten planets, and each suit of the minor arcana is linked with one of the four elements.

Astrological Associations of the Major Arcana

CARD	ASSOCIATION	SYMBOL
THE FOOL	Uranus	♅
THE MAGICIAN	Mercury	☿
THE HIGH PRIESTESS	Moon	☽
THE EMPRESS	Venus	♀
THE EMPEROR	Aries	♈
THE HIEROPHANT	Taurus	♉
THE LOVERS	Gemini	♊
THE CHARIOT	Cancer	♋
JUSTICE	Libra	♌
THE HERMIT	Virgo	♍
THE WHEEL OF FORTUNE	Jupiter	♃
STRENGTH	Leo	♎
THE HANGED MAN	Neptune	♆
DEATH	Scorpio	♏
TEMPERANCE	Sagittarius	♐
THE DEVIL	Capricorn	♑
THE TOWER	Mars	♂
THE STAR	Aquarius	♒
THE MOON	Pisces	♓
THE SUN	Sun	☉
JUDGMENT	Pluto	♇
THE WORLD	Saturn	♄

Astrological Associations of the Minor Arcana

SUIT	Cups	Wands	Coins	Swords
AREA OF INFLUENCE	Emotions	Career	Material matters	Intellectual/spiritual concerns
ELEMENT	Water	Fire	Earth	Air
SYMBOL	▽	△	▢	◡

When we look back into the history of humanity, we can see that magic has always played a key role in the way that humans live. Primitive man lived in fear of storms, lightning, floods, and drought, and would use magical means to propitiate the forces of nature.

THE PRACTICE OF MAGIC

Whenever decisions needed to be made, ancient tribes would seek guidance from sorcerers, who were able to commune with the spirit world. In Celtic Europe, for example, it was the Druids who exercised sway over the minds of the people; and in every place in the world, there is evidence of such "interveners with the gods."

As tribal society grew into countries, and economic development and trade began, magical practice turned into religion, which is still ultimately a way in which we attempt to persuade our gods to grant us certain things that we are unable to control ourselves. It could be said in this regard that prayer is a form of magic.

CAUSE AND EFFECT

The essential difference between religion and magic is that, with the former, we are expected to have faith; that is, a belief in something that we do not really experience and know for ourselves to be true. In magic, no belief is necessary, and rather than accepting the will of some deity or spirit greater than ourselves, we attempt to direct spiritual forces in the way that we wish to see them move. Magic is far more self-directional, far more causative. It places the responsibility for the outcomes of one's life directly in the hands of those who practice it. So, magic we can then define as a causative approach to life.

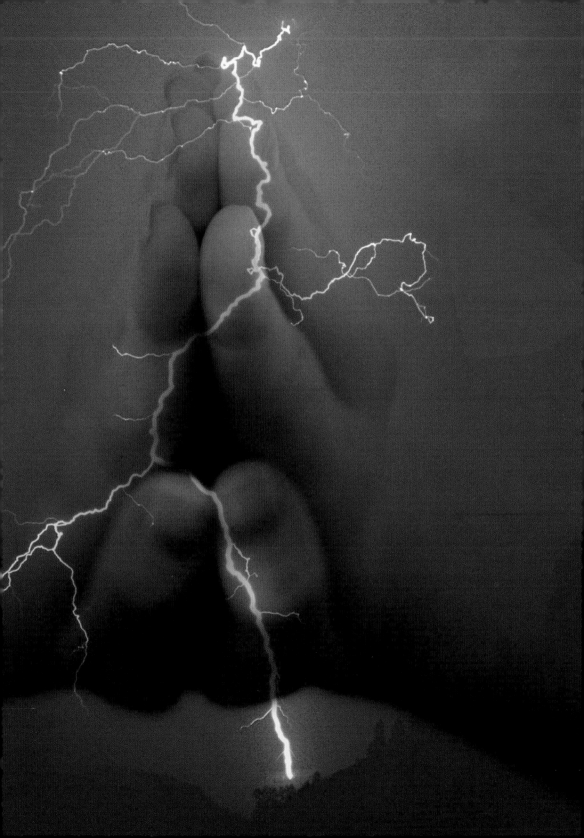

TAROT SPELLCASTING

The word "spell" derives from ancient times when the wise woman or man of the tribe would cast rune stones upon the ground and read what they "spelled" out. A runic letter was carved on each small stone, each letter meaning something specific, such as "arrow," "oxen," "gift," and so on. By "reading" how the letters fell, she or he would be able to determine the will of the gods in a particular instance.

The symbols that we see on tarot cards are simply more sophisticated versions of these crude carvings in stone. The whole spectrum of spiritual realities is represented in the symbols of the major arcana, and every conceivable scenario or experience is represented in the minor arcana.

The tarot is generally used for divinatory purposes;
that is, an attempt to understand what has gone before
and discover what the options might be for the future.
The person having the reading receives a kind of
reprogramming that prepares him or her for certain
events, and creates expectations in his or her unconscious
mind. In a sense, a tarot reading is a spell.

This book takes tarot spellcrafting to a higher level.
The tarot deck becomes our basic instrument, and is
used to create incredible experiences for those who are
prepared to try it. What we are doing in casting a magic
spell is reaching around the rim of time and transferring
something that we are karmically entitled to from
a future time period to the present. Thus, there
is no way we can ever bring anything to ourselves
through magic to which we are not entitled.
What we are able to do is activate latent karma
and bring benefits into our lives sooner than
would otherwise occur.

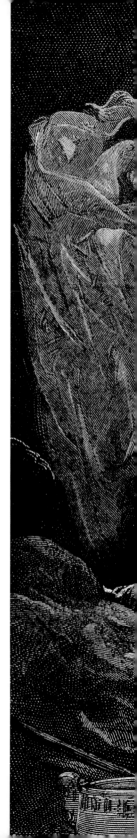

Although some people believe that it is wrong to use magic to influence events, most agree that it is perfectly acceptable to use magic to take greater control over one's life as long as the free will of others is not impinged upon. Most agree that you should ask permission before casting a spell for someone else.

THE ETHICS OF MAGIC

BLACK MAGIC

The basic intention of magic should be to bring about greater freedom, love, and happiness. When hatred is the emotion used to instigate negative changes in the lives of others, this is often called black magic. When an individual moves down this path, he or she sows the seeds of his or her own destruction.

Black magic not only uses magical forces for selfish ends, but is also generated by emotions such as hatred, fear, and ignorance, and has as its ultimate aim the harming and destruction of humanity. Those who choose to practice such magic may experience short-term gains; they may well get their revenge or attain wealth very quickly. However, in a relatively short space of time, the negative forces they are sending out will return and act against them, but even stronger.

LOVE SPELLS

One of the most popular types of spell is the love spell, but to use magic to make a particular person fall in love with you is something that you should avoid. Instead, it is better to invite an unknown lover, your soul mate, to come into your life. The spiritual forces that you set in motion through the use of magic may well have someone else in mind than the person you desire, someone who would be far better for you in the long run.

You might well be able to draw the person you desire to you, but think for a moment—just how well do you know him or her? A wiser policy is to let the identity of your future lover be determined by the higher spiritual forces that watch over us, and guide us whenever we give them the chance. To interfere with the free will of another for our own gratification takes us close to black magic, no matter how much we may feel justified in doing so, or how desperate we may be.

KEEPING a magical DIARY

You might like to maintain a magical diary once you begin spellcasting, in which you keep a record of your thoughts, dreams, hopes, and fears, as well as the spells you perform. It will help you maintain a greater sense of control over your magical workings. When people are new to magic, they can become swept up in their own enthusiasm, and end up in a realm in which everything is suddenly magical. This is a route to instability. Keeping a diary will help you maintain a sense of balance and control over how your life is unfolding in response to the magic you are making. Knowledge, like power, is nothing without control.

A magical diary also gives a sense of perspective, in that you can look back and see the correlation between a particular spell that has been cast and the result that was achieved. Without keeping tabs on the causes and the effects, you will never really know whether something has worked or not. In addition, as your practice of magic evolves, you will start to see the world differently, and your diary will provide precious recollections for you to look back on.

Before beginning your spellcasting, you should spend some time creating the right physical atmosphere. Always make sure you have everything you will need for the spell at hand. This includes a consecrated tarot deck, some magical tools, and any special ingredients listed in the spell. You may also like to dress in special robes. When you have everything ready, set up your altar and begin.

PREPARING FOR SPELLCASTING

WEARING SPECIAL ROBES

You may find it helpful to wear special robes during your spellcasting. A simple, T-shaped, ankle-length robe is very easy to make. You can make several robes in your favorite colors, or perhaps wear colors to match the altar cloths recommended in the spells. Although they are not vital, robes can help you achieve a magical state of mind by divorcing you from the ordinary, mundane world. Some people regard wearing robes as a sign of respect and honor for the practice of magic. After all, if you were practicing karate, you would invest in a special suit of clothing.

magical t⊕⊕ls

The four basic tools used on the tarot altar are a knife or censer to represent the Suit of Swords, a wand or candlestick to symbolize the Suit of Wands, a cup or glass to represent the Suit of Cups, and a coin or crystal to symbolize the Suit of Coins. These will help you connect more closely with the symbolism of the tarot. It is worth spending some time and perhaps money on finding appropriately beautiful objects. Although not vital, this will help to show your respect for the power of the forces you are intending to direct through your magical work.

You can keep your magical tools as symbolic objects, or utilize them in the spells if you wish. For example, if a spell requires that you inscribe words into a candle, you could use your magical knife to do so. Similarly, if a glass of water is needed, you could pour the water into your magical cup or glass. Always keep your tools separate from those things you use in your everyday life, and care for them well. It is a good idea to store them in a special spell box by the side of your altar when not in use.

INGREDIENTS
FOR SPELLS

For each of the spells in this book, you will find a list of ingredients, including particular altar cloth colors, candles, and essential oils, as well as objects such as mirrors, coins, and foods. Although magic is really about harnessing the power of your own unconscious mind, the use of these ingredients is a way of encouraging this to happen. If you cannot find the exact ingredients recommended, apply a little common sense and choose suitable alternatives. For example, if you cannot find rose essential oil for a love spell, choose another oil with a heady, flowery scent. You should also feel free to decorate your altar with any other items that seem appropriate. For example, if a spell uses jasmine oil, you might like to scatter jasmine petals on the altar. When you have finished casting a spell, let the candles and/or incense burn for as long as you have time, unless indicated otherwise (do not leave them burning unattended).

TALISMANS AND AMULETS

It is important to keep all the talismans and amulets you make along the way.
An amulet is a three-dimensional object, such as a stone or coin, that represents
your magical purposes. A talisman is a two-dimensional object, such as a piece
of parchment with something written on it, to attract certain influences or
repel others. You must exercise control over any items you make. To leave
them lying around for children to play with, or anyone else for that matter, is not
good practice. They represent significant stages of your own development, and they
contain considerable quantities of your personal life force. Always treat them with
respect; a good idea is to store them in your spell box alongside your magical tools.

Some of the spells prompt you to carry a talisman or amulet with you at certain
times. To do this, you could make an uanga bag to hold them. An uanga bag is the
African name for a pouch containing magical objects that is hung around the neck.

DRESSING CANDLES

To dress a candle means to anoint it with oil. In doing so, you
consecrate it for magical use. Place a little essential oil on your
index finger. Starting at the middle of each candle, take the oil
up to the top, then straight down to the bottom, then up to
the middle again, twisting the candle as you go.

CONSECRATING
YOUR TAROT CARDS

You can work with any deck of tarot cards you prefer—
simply choose the ones you like the look of, or that
seem most appropriate to the spell you wish to cast.
Most people settle on a couple of different decks that
they like to work with. When not in use, store the
cards safely, perhaps in a velvet pouch in your spell box.
Never allow anyone else to touch your tarot cards.

Before using a deck of cards for the first time, it is a
good idea to consecrate them. To do this, spread them
face up across a table, or even the floor (which must be
clean). Holding a bottle of lavender essential oil in one
hand, place your other hand over it, and recite:

*May the power of universal good bless this oil, as a symbol of my intention to study,
learn, and train, and may my actions, thoughts, and words be guided by this power.*

Pour a little oil onto the fingertips of one hand, then pick
up the cards with your other hand, one by one. Spread a
very thin layer of oil over the surface of each card, taking
care not to put too much on them. If you do, you will
create a mess and find that the cards stick together.

As you go through the deck, look at the stories being
told in the images on the cards. Reflect on the good times
you have enjoyed in your own life so far, and also the
times of sadness and regret. Let yourself be moved by
whatever tears or laughter happens to surface through
this process. As you oil the court cards (the king, queen,
knight, and page), you may find yourself thinking about
some of the people you have known in the past. You
might like to wonder about the people who will play a
significant role in your life in the future. What might they
look like? What might life be like when you meet them?
Take a look—what do you see?

THE TAROT ALTAR

An altar acts as a kind of radio transmitter between you and the magical realm. You can use an ordinary table or chest. The most effective altars are usually the simplest; the purity of the design seems to maintain the potency of the magic. The more detailed your altar, the more you may be distracted by it. Remember that the altar is for your own personal use. It is not there to impress others with its grandiosity.

Use a compass to ascertain the directions north, south, east, and west. If you do not have a compass, approximate the four points based on the direction in which the sun rises (east). Starting in the east, mark out the elemental symbols for each direction on the tabletop (see chart below); either draw them directly on the altar with chalk or on pieces of parchment or paper. As you do so, invoke the presence of the archangel that governs each direction by reciting the appropriate name, slowly and with deep resonance.

Lay a cloth on the table. It can be a small cloth in the center or a large cloth that drapes over the sides of the altar. It does not matter if it covers the symbols you have drawn; the important thing is that you know they are

COMPASS DIRECTION	East	South	West	North
ELEMENT	Air	Fire	Water	Earth
ELEMENTAL SYMBOL	◯	△	▽	⊡
ARCHANGEL AND HIS ASSOCIATIONS	Raphael—golden yellow; strong winds, racing clouds	Michael—deep reds; surging flames, erupting volcanoes	Gabriel—blues and grays; great waves, waterfalls, driving rain	Uriel—browns and greens; lush foliage, birds and animals
TAROT SYMBOL	Suit of Swords— knife or censer	Suit of Wands— wand or candlestick	Suit of Cups— cup or glass	Suit of Coins— coin or crystal
REALM OF INFLUENCE	Thought	Energy	Time	Matter

there, harnessing the power of the elements for your magic. Place the appropriate tarot symbol (your magical tools) at each of the compass directions (see chart below left). As you do so, visualize the four archangels standing around the circle, looking down at you. Feel their piercing eyes and thoughts as they scan you, ascertaining the purity of your intentions.

When you are ready to begin spellcasting, return your magical tools to their storage box or leave them on the altar, either to use in the spell or for decoration. If the spell requires lots of ingredients, it may be best to remove them. When you have finished a spell, leave everything in place on the altar for at least one night before dismantling it. Some spells involve leaving specific items on the altar as a thanksgiving; if you wish, you can do this for all the spells—some candy and a glass of wine make good offerings.

Before casting a spell, it is a good idea to try some meditation exercises to help you relax and achieve the right magical state of mind. Similarly, using such exercises to close the spiritual faculties after a spellcasting is also important.

ACHIEVING a MAGICAL MINDSET

TAROT MEDITATION

Make the room as comfortable as possible and sit in front of your altar, with your magical tools in front of you. As well as representing the four suits of the minor arcana, these items also symbolize the four elements of time, matter, thought, and energy. Sit and enjoy the experience of getting into your mode of magician. You should have fun with this; magic is there to be enjoyed.

Let your thoughts run through your mind, and try to recall a pleasant experience. Part of the art of magic is being aware of where your thoughts are taking you, and every now and again consciously influencing the direction they are heading. Imagine yourself walking in a beautiful place. The smells, sights, and sounds of this place are sweet, and known only to you. Open up communication with all the creatures you meet there. You will find that some of this communication is emotional rather than verbal. What you are doing is creating a link between your conscious and unconscious mind, and thereby the collective unconscious mind to which we are all linked.

OPENING THE
THIRD EYE

You are now ready to open your "Third Eye"; that is, your
ability to see into the spirit world. One way of doing this
is by imagining a thread of color moving up your spine,
over the top of your head, and then down over your
forehead. It stops right between your eyes, just above
the brow of the nose. Bring this place to life by imagining
it as a tiny flower, slowly opening like a bud to the light
around it. Spend some time doing this, and allow it to
open at its own natural rate. It might or might not open
fully at first; but as you practice, you will find that the
sensation of increasing awareness unfolds more rapidly.
You might like to imagine that you can actually see
through this new aperture.

INVOKING YOUR GUARDIAN ANGEL

The invocation of one's guardian angel is an ancient practice that goes back to Old Testament times. If you send out messages of love from deep within your heart, you can invite your guardian angel to appear before you, so that you can communicate directly with it and benefit from its wisdom during your spellcasting. Basically, this is a good way of encouraging the forces of light and truth into your life. You can then achieve a closer connection with the forces of universal good before setting out on the road of magic. At the very least, it is an insurance policy that is always worth investing in.

BREATHING

You can slow down the speed of your thoughts by breathing more deeply and more slowly. If you find that you are getting anxious or uncomfortable at any point during a spellcasting, then by making a minor adjustment to your breathing you will be able to change your mood, and start to enjoy yourself and your magic once more.

This easy-to-use spellfinder will help you find
the most appropriate spell for your needs.

THE SPELLFINDER

HEALTH AND HAPPINESS

Physical health:	The Empress Spell p44
	Temperance Spell p66
	The Tower Spell p70
	The Moon Spell p74
	The Sun Spell p76
Psychological health:	Temperance Spell p66
	The Moon Spell p74
Happiness:	The Empress Spell p44
	Justice Spell p54
	The Wheel of Fortune Spell p58
	Spell for Adventures in Life p86
Admiration and respect:	The Magician Spell p40
	The Hierophant Spell p48
	The Hermit Spell p56
	The Wheel of Fortune Spell p58
	Strength Spell p60
	The World Spell p80
	Spell for the Admiration of Others p84
	Spell for Interview Success p92
	Spell for Friendship p98

NEW HORIZONS

New opportunities:	The Fool Spell p38
	The Wheel of Fortune Spell p58
	Death Spell p64
	The Tower Spell p70
	Spell for Adventures in Life p86
	Spell for Self-empowerment p118
Travel:	The Fool Spell p38
	The Magician Spell p40
	The Hermit Spell p56
	The Wheel of Fortune Spell p58
	The Sun Spell p76
	The World Spell p80

HIDDEN KNOWLEDGE

Magical powers:	The High Priestess Spell p42
	The Hierophant Spell p48
	Strength Spell p60
	Spell for Self-protection p116
	Spell for Self-initiation p120
	Spell for Gaining Magical Knowledge p124
Intuition:	The High Priestess Spell p42
Discovering secrets:	The High Priestess Spell p42
	The Hermit Spell p56
	The Moon Spell p74
	Spell for Uncovering Secrets p122

SUCCESS

Business:	The Magician Spell p40
	The Wheel of Fortune Spell p58
	Strength Spell p60
	The World Spell p80
	Spell for Interview Success p92
Examinations and competitive situations:	The Magician Spell p40
	The Emperor Spell p46
	The Hierophant Spell p48
	Strength Spell p60
	Spell for Passing Examinations p94
	Spell for Passing a Driving Test p96
Legal:	The Magician Spell p40
	Justice Spell p54
	Spell for Settling Disputes p110

PROTECTION

Personal:	The Chariot Spell p52
	The Hermit Spell p56
	The Moon Spell p74
	The World Spell p80
	Spell for Self-protection p116
Loved ones:	The Chariot Spell p52
	The Tower Spell p70
	The Moon Spell p74
	The Sun Spell p76
	The World Spell p80
	Spell for Protecting Children p112
Home:	The Chariot Spell p52
	The Wheel of Fortune Spell p58
	The Sun Spell p76
	Spell for Protecting the Home p114
Financial:	The Magician Spell p40
	The Wheel of Fortune Spell p58
	The Tower Spell p70

SELF-DEVELOPMENT

Self-esteem:	The Emperor Spell p46
	Strength Spell p60
	The Devil Spell p68
	The Star Spell p72
	Judgment Spell p78
	Spell for Adventures in Life p86
	Spell for Self-empowerment p118
Creativity:	The Magician Spell p40
	The Empress Spell p44
	The Hermit Spell p56
	The Star Spell p72
	Spell for Passing Examinations p94
	Spell for Self-empowerment p118
Insight:	The Fool Spell p38
	The Hanged Man Spell p62
	Temperance Spell p66
	Spell for Self-initiation p120
	Spell for Uncovering Secrets p122
	Spell for Gaining Magical Knowledge p124
Positive characteristics:	The High Priestess Spell p42
	The Wheel of Fortune Spell p58

PROBLEMS

Removing negative influences:	The Fool Spell p38
	The Emperor Spell p46
	Death Spell p64
	The Devil Spell p68
	Judgment Spell p78
	Spell for Getting Rid of a Lover p106
	Spell for Vanquishing Troublesome People p108
	Spell for Self-protection p116
Making a decision:	The Lovers Spell p50
	The Hermit Spell p56
	The Hanged Man Spell p62
Winning a battle:	The Emperor Spell p46
	The Tower Spell p70
	Spell for Settling Disputes p110

LOVE

Attracting love:	The Empress Spell p44
	The Lovers Spell p50
	The Moon Spell p74
	Spell for Enhancing Love p100
	Spell for Passionate Encounters p104
Fidelity:	The Lovers Spell p50
	Spell for Getting Rid of a Lover p106
Fertility:	The Empress Spell p44

WEALTH

Material:	The Magician Spell p40
	The High Priestess Spell p42
	The Wheel of Fortune Spell p58
	The Sun Spell p76
	Judgment Spell p78
	The World Spell p80
	Spell for the Admiration of Others p84
	Spell for the Riches of the Earth p88
Emotional:	Judgment Spell p78
	Spell for the Admiration of Others p84
Spiritual:	Justice Spell p54
	Judgment Spell p78

This chapter contains one spell for each card of the major arcana. Choose which spell to cast based on the outcome you desire. Alternately, meditate on the state of your life at this moment in time, shuffle the major arcana cards, then choose a card at random and cast the spell for this card. Another option is to work your way through each spell in turn over a period of time, to symbolize your journey along the tree of life.

THE MAJOR ARCANA

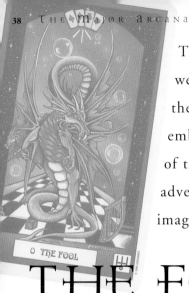

0 THE FOOL

The Fool travels along the road of experience, welcoming new encounters. Connected with Uranus, the Fool is related in mythology to all those who embark on fantastical quests—he is Jason in search of the Golden Fleece. He can lead us forward into new adventures, and open doorways that previously we had not imagined existed. The Fool is the genius within each of us.

THE FOOL SPELL

MAGICAL INTENTION

To break down barriers that have grown around you; to open the doorway to new and interesting experiences, relationships, and ways of thinking; to embark on new travels and business opportunities.

MAGICAL WORKING

Inscribe your name along the side of the red candle, then dress the candle with cinnamon oil. Place the candle in the east of the altar, and light it. Inscribe the following words along the side of the white candle: "Freedom, Joy, Happiness." Dress the candle with sandalwood oil, then place it in the west of the altar, and light it. Lay the Fool card between the two candles, and holding both hands over it, recite:

In the name of the forces of light, I hereby consecrate my life's experience, so that it shall be filled with freedom, happiness, and joy, and that in so living, I shall be a beacon of encouragement to others. Let the power of light shine through all my workings. I am the Fool, he is in me, and I in him. So mote it be.

Visualize yourself dressed as the Fool, and concentrate on building circles of colored light around you. Imagine these lights shooting off in all directions throughout the universe. Pick up the cord, tie it into a knot, then carefully cut through the knot, saying:

Let this cord represent all that has ever held me back, and let this act of magical intention represent the road to freedom that now opens before me.

Seal the cut ends of the cord with some molten wax from each candle, then store the pieces in a safe place as an amulet.

YOU WILL NEED

Green altar cloth ❶
Knife ❷
Red candle ❸
Cinnamon essential oil ❹
White candle ❺
Sandalwood essential oil ❻
The Fool card ❼
Length of cord ❽

The Magician, also known as the Cobbler or Juggler, relates to the legends of Thoth Tehuti in the Egyptian pantheon, Hermes in the Greek pantheon, and Mercury in the Roman pantheon. He is the lord of communication, bringing messages to mortals from the higher realms. It is through him that we are able to classify and analyze diverse phenomena.

THE MAGICIAN SPELL

YOU WILL NEED

White altar cloth ❶
The Magician card ❷
Two yellow or white candles ❸
Cinnamon or clove essential oil and oil burner ❹
Parchment or paper ❺
Pen or paintbrush with red ink or paint ❻
Drawstring pouch ❼

MAGICAL INTENTION

To secure success in contracts, finances, acquisitions, examinations, and business; for protection against fraud or embezzlement, success in legal entanglements, and victory in court decisions; for increased writing skills and foreign travel; for the ability to influence others favorably, particularly those with influence over you, or who are in a position to bring benefits, material or otherwise, into your life.

MAGICAL WORKING

Lay the Magician card in the center of the altar, between two lit yellow or white candles. Place the oil burner containing the essential oil in the north of the altar and light it. Visualize your seating area becoming surrounded by a wonderful circle of yellow light, with yourself at the center. Starting as a small point of light, you see a figure-eight pattern emerge and flow around the edges of the circle. As it does so, the circle solidifies into a three-dimensional sphere of light, like a miniature sun, resplendent and radiating security, harmony, and intelligence. On a piece of parchment, use red ink or paint to draw the symbol for Mercury in red (pictured above right). Carefully fold or roll up the symbol and place it in the pouch as a talisman. Wear this around your neck or carry it with you in a pocket or purse until you are satisfied with the success you have achieved. To enhance its efficacy, dab some of the essential oil onto the pouch for several days after performing the spell.

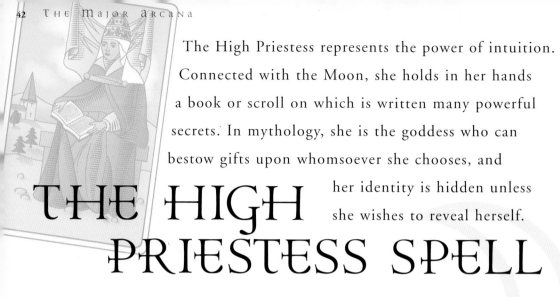

The High Priestess represents the power of intuition. Connected with the Moon, she holds in her hands a book or scroll on which is written many powerful secrets. In mythology, she is the goddess who can bestow gifts upon whomsoever she chooses, and her identity is hidden unless she wishes to reveal herself.

THE HIGH PRIESTESS SPELL

MAGICAL INTENTION

To activate your powers of intuition; to uncover secrets, especially the secret desires of others; to discover where riches are hidden; to develop your counseling and healing abilities; to gain entry into the world of magical forces.

YOU WILL NEED

Dark blue altar cloth ❶
Black candle ❷
White candle ❸
Frankincense essential oil and oil burner ❹
The High Priestess card ❺
White chalk or length of white cord ❻
Small mirror ❼

MAGICAL WORKING

Place the black candle in the east of the altar, the white candle in the west, and light them. Put the oil burner containing essential oil in the north of the altar and light it. Lay the High Priestess card between the two candles, and recite:

Blessed be my mind, which shall realize great thoughts. Blessed be my eyes, which shall look upon all the heavens. Blessed be my ears, which shall hear the words of the god and goddess. Blessed be my loins, which shall connect with the earthly realms into which I have been born. Blessed be my feet, which shall walk with the guidance and guardianship of the higher powers.

As you recite each sentence, touch the appropriate body part with both palms. With the piece of chalk, draw a spiral from the feet of the High Priestess downward to the outer rim of the altar cloth. Alternately, use a piece of white cord to form the spiral. Make sure that each circle of the spiral is slightly larger than the last. As the oil burns, visualize your thoughts, hopes, and aspirations rising up to a higher realm.

Gaze into the mirror, and imagine that you see the room behind you turning a bluish hue, and that there is a silvery moon hanging from above. Picture the image of the High Priestess superimposed upon your own face, and open a conversation with her. Ask her what you will. You will be given the answers you need.

The Empress is a radiant, beautiful woman, filled with purity and divine love. She can soothe away the heartbreak of a lifetime, and impart a sense of lightness and fulfillment into the hearts of others. In mythology she is Venus, the goddess of love, and she can bestow love on whomever she pleases.

THE EMPRESS SPELL

MAGICAL INTENTION

To ease the heart of sadness, regrets, and disillusionment; to create complimentary energies for becoming pregnant; to feel young and revitalized; to ignite the flame of personal creativity; to receive an abundance of love.

YOU WILL NEED

1. Dark green altar cloth
2. Knife
3. Orange candle
4. Bergamot essential oil
5. Light green candle
6. Frankincense essential oil
7. The Empress card
8. Seashells
9. Flowers

MAGICAL WORKING

Inscribe your name along the side of the orange candle, dress it with bergamot oil, then place it in the east of the altar and light it. Inscribe the following words along the side of the light green candle: "Love, Abundance, Love." Dress this candle with frankincense oil, then place it in the west of the altar and light it. Lay the Empress card between the two candles, study the card for a few moments, then recite:

Let this card represent the power of the goddess of love, and may this spiritual being look upon me as a fitting receptacle for blessing. May the energies of love, creativity, and harmony flow into and through my life from this point forward and for all time. So mote it be.

Take the seashells in your left hand, and the flowers in your right hand, and walk clockwise around the altar three times. At each of the compass points, pause, face outward from the altar, and bow your head, as if the goddess were approaching from each of the directions. Imagine that the air around you is a vibrant golden white, and picture this energy flowing directly into your heart. Allow yourself to feel a sense of warmth, release, and completion. Face the altar again, and while looking at the Empress, pass your hands filled with shells and flowers from the tip of your head, down over your body, to your toes. As you do so, visualize the cleansing effect that the shells and flowers are having on your aura.

Associated with Aries, the mighty Emperor is a man who can take responsibility and make important decisions. He represents the warrior in each of us, for in a sense each of our lives is a story of struggling for freedom from the constraints that others might like to set around us. As well as a bringer of war, he is also the establisher of a lasting peace based on real justice.

THE EMPEROR SPELL

MAGICAL INTENTION

To increase assertiveness, effectiveness, and leadership abilities; to achieve a more independent lifestyle; to succeed in a new project where there is likely to be conflict with others; for victory in all of life's battles.

MAGICAL WORKING

Dress both candles with oil, then place one in the east of the altar and one in the west. Lay the Emperor card between them, and light the candles. Place the tobacco in a censer or oil burner in the north of the altar and light it; the tobacco plant is sacred to Mars. When you have done this, walk around the altar in a clockwise direction. At each of the compass points, draw the symbol of Aries (pictured above right) in the air with the knife. Return to your starting position and recite:

I hereby invoke the power of the Emperor, lord of armies, to be my shield and my sword in the battles that lie ahead. Let my arm be strong and grant that I may fight a good battle. So mote it be.

Facing inward, look at the Emperor and think back to some of the battles you have faced in the past. In particular, think about setbacks and opponents. Now visualize a huge giant facing those same opponents. See them running from the giant, their ranks breaking as their armies are dashed to pieces. Picture this giant standing on the opposite side of the altar. Both of you lean forward until your heads touch and begin to merge together. When this has happened, allow the giant to straighten up, this time taking your head with him, up onto his shoulders. Look around you from your new perspective on top of the giant's shoulders. Who can stand against you now?·

YOU WILL NEED

Red altar cloth ❶
Two red candles ❷
Sunflower oil ❸
The Emperor card ❹
Pinch of tobacco and
censer or oil burner ❺
Knife ❻

The Hierophant, also known as the Pope, represents spiritual power on the earthly plane, and holds the keys to heaven and hell. Connected with Taurus, he is a teacher who brings his students along the road of knowledge, carefully preparing them to take on responsibilities as they learn from him.

THE HIEROPHANT SPELL

MAGICAL INTENTION

To gain greater knowledge of the mysteries of life and death; to succeed in educational activities and examinations; to gain the respect and admiration of others.

YOU WILL NEED

Gold altar cloth **1**
Knife **2**
Two orange candles **3**
Frankincense essential oil **4**
The Hierophant card **5**
Parchment or paper **6**
Pen or paintbrush with red ink or paint **7**

MAGICAL WORKING

Inscribe your name along the side of both candles, then dress them with oil. Place one candle in the east of the altar and one in the west, and light them. Lay the Hierophant card between them and recite:

I hereby invoke the power of the Hierophant. May he be present in all my undertakings, by night and by day, and may he make my life a place of refuge from the storm. Master teacher, grant that I shall prove a good student to your teachings, so that I in turn may teach and inspire others, who in turn shall teach and inspire future generations. So mote it be.

Visualize concentric circles of light emanating from your altar, out into space, in all directions. As you see this happen, notice that they take on different colors; do not try to make them any particular color. On the piece of parchment, draw the symbol for Taurus (pictured above right) in red. Concentrate all the circles of light going into the symbol, then visualize a wise and learned teacher coming along a road to meet you. Look into his face. In your imagination, step into his world, and let him take you with him. When you return, maintain the sense of his presence around you. Keep the parchment near you as a talisman so that you can access this energy whenever you need guidance and direction.

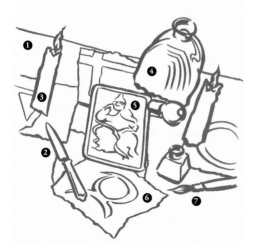

The theme of the Lovers appears in all the world's mythology, as well as in contemporary literature and movies. Associated with Gemini, the Lovers represent the story of two people who find true love after many trials and testing experiences. Together, they can overcome the obstacles that other people place around them.

THE LOVERS SPELL

MAGICAL INTENTION

To attract your soul mate; to attract more love into your life in general; to make the right decision about a relationship problem; to ensure your partner's fidelity.

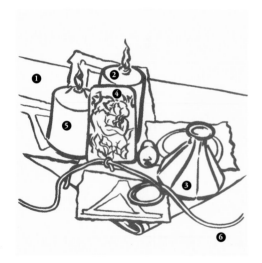

MAGICAL WORKING

Dress the gold candle with oil, place it in the center of the altar, and light it. This candle represents the golden charisma you possess inside, which this spell will reveal to your soul mate. Rest the Lovers card upright against the candle. Dress the green candle with oil and light it. Hold the candle up in front of you, close your eyes, and imagine the qualities you would like in a lover. Place the green candle beside the gold one so that they are touching and recite:

I hereby invoke the power of the Lovers. May they be present in my life at this point, may they participate in my relationship choices, and may my life become filled with abundant love. In the name of the archangel Gabriel, so mote it be.

YOU WILL NEED

Gold altar cloth ❶
Gold candle ❷
Rose essential oil ❸
The Lovers card ❹
Green candle ❺
Two lengths of red cord ❻

Tie the two lengths of cord together, and imagine yourself and another person being linked by some binding agency, out on the astral plane. Visualize meeting each other in a gamut of guises and situations—going for a walk together, swimming, eating out, staying in, making love, and so on. Make the images as big and as bright as you can. As the candles burn down, continue to see the other person near you. Keep the tied lengths of cord in a safe place as an amulet.

The Chariot is linked with concentration and direction of energy. In ancient times the chariot was the quickest and most effective way of moving fighting men from one position to another, so the Chariot represents the power to defend ourselves and respond to threats. It is also linked with the astrological sign of Cancer, which symbolizes the home and motherhood.

VII THE CHARIOT

THE CHARIOT SPELL

MAGICAL INTENTION

To secure your personal boundaries and achieve greater safety and security; for protection before embarking on a hazardous mission; to safeguard mothers, children, and the home.

MAGICAL WORKING

YOU WILL NEED

White altar cloth ❶
Two blue candles ❷
Rosemary essential oil ❸
The Chariot card ❹
Length of chain ❺

Dress both candles with oil, place one in the east of the altar and one in the west, and light them. Lay the Chariot card between them, close your eyes, and hold both hands directly over it. Be silent for a few minutes, then open your eyes and recite:

I hereby summon the power of the Chariot, to be with me and to participate in all my activities in whatever way it so chooses. With thanks and in appreciation, so mote it be.

Visualize energy from your hands flowing down into the card, and see the suggestion of movement in the image. As you breathe, pull in the energy from the air around you, and let it flow down through your body and from your hands. Imagine a golden disk hovering above your head. Let your head open up, and allow this disk to move inside your head, through your body, and out through your hands. See the golden light encompassing the Chariot.

Tell the charioteer who requires protection and against what. He is one of the most powerful protective spirits. Picture him embarking on his mission, and thank him for coming to you and pledging his service. Do not call on him too frequently, or trouble him with petty matters, because he may become angry and refuse his help. As an offering to him, place a length of chain on the altar. Leave it there for two or three days after the spell has been cast, then bury it at a crossroads.

Justice is depicted holding a scale, in which to weigh the transgressor against his or her sins. She also possesses a double-edged sword, one edge to deal out punishment and the other edge to save. She is connected with Libra, and symbolizes balance and harmony.

XI JUSTICE

JUSTICE SPELL

MAGICAL INTENTION

To secure fairness in a legal problem, lawsuit, or divorce settlement; to improve your karma and gain your just desserts.

MAGICAL WORKING

Dress both candles with oil, place the white candle in the east of the altar and the black candle in the west, then light them. Lay the Justice card between them, and focusing your mind on the matter troubling you, gaze into the card for around fifteen to twenty minutes. Think about it in as much detail as possible, including its origins and possible outcomes. Make sure you spend the full amount of time doing this. Write down everything that comes to mind if you find it helpful.

When you are finished, pick up the length of cord, and with one hand behind your back and the other hand up above your shoulder, hold the cord so that it runs behind you between both hands. Pull the cord with alternate hands. As you pull with the lower hand, notice that it pulls down uncomfortably on the upper hand, and vice versa. This is the point. Whatever situation you are in, the only way you can change things is by taking responsibility for having allowed it to happen. That may be by omission rather than commission, but by taking responsibility you take control. Now you realize that you do not have to pull one hand against the other.

Using red ink, write down on the parchment what it is that you would like to be experiencing in a year's time. Write in as much detail as you can. Place the parchment inside the envelope, seal it, and keep it safe for one year. (It is best to do this spell on New Year's Eve.) After a year has passed, open the envelope. You will be amazed at just how much has come to pass.

YOU WILL NEED

Dark green altar cloth **1**
White candle **2**
Black candle **3**
Ylang-ylang essential oil **4**
Justice card **5**
Length of cord **6**
Pen with red ink **7**
Parchment or paper **8**
Envelope **9**

Connected with Virgo, the Hermit symbolizes the journey in search of enlightenment. Often he represents God moving upon the face of the world, testing the people he meets, rewarding those who treat him with charity, and punishing those who try to make him suffer.

THE HERMIT SPELL

MAGICAL INTENTION

To uncover hidden secrets; to discover the causes of things; to develop your critical and analytical faculties; for protection against gossip; for a good reputation and the regard of those in authority; for interesting encounters while traveling; for enhanced ability to make shrewd decisions that will affect your life in important ways.

MAGICAL WORKING

Dress the white candle with essential oil, place it in the north of the altar, and light it. Put the feather in the east of the altar, the eggcup of olive oil in the south, and the hourglass in the west. Rest the Hermit card upright against the candle. Dip the feather into the olive oil and wipe a small smear on your forehead. Dip the feather into the oil again and sprinkle droplets around the altar in a clockwise direction. Replace the feather and turn over the hourglass, so that the sand begins running through the narrow channel.

Visualize yourself as a tree, with the roots deepening into the earth, and the branches reaching far up into the sky. Feel the wind on your arms, and imagine that fruit of many kinds is growing from your fingers. Underneath your toes you can sense tiny animals burrowing into the ground; it may even feel ticklish. Focus on the image on the card, and allow it to grow, until finally the Hermit walks out of the card and into the room in front of you. Allow him to walk right into you physically. He has now become part of you. When all the sand has run through the hourglass, sprinkle some salt around the rim of the altar, working in a clockwise direction.

YOU WILL NEED

Gray altar cloth ❶
White candle ❷
Myrrh essential oil ❸
Feather ❹
Eggcup of olive oil ❺
Hourglass ❻
The Hermit card ❼
Salt ❽

ROUE DE FORTUNE

The Wheel of Fortune is connected with the cyclical pattern of life and death. Associated with Jupiter, a symbol of generosity and abundance, the best place to be is at the center of the Wheel. Whoever sits there is unaffected by the impostors of success and failure.

THE WHEEL OF FORTUNE SPELL

MAGICAL INTENTION

To develop generosity, compassion, and cheerfulness in the face of adversity; for success, abundance, and new business and travel possibilities; to gain the applause of the crowd; to safeguard investments, especially property.

MAGICAL WORKING

Place the candles on the altar in the form of an equilateral triangle—one in the north, one in the southeast, and one in the southwest. Lay the Wheel of Fortune card and the oil burner containing essential oil within the triangle of candles. Light the oil burner, and as its wisps of aroma begin to rise, imagine that your desires rise up with them. Spend a few moments thinking about what you would like to happen, then recite:

May the mighty creative powers of the universe smile upon me, and grant me the blessings that this world has to offer. May my life become richly rewarded, and may I be loved and admired for the wonderful person I really am. So mote it be.

YOU WILL NEED
Red altar cloth ❶
Three blue candles ❷
The Wheel of Fortune card ❸
Frankincense essential oil and oil burner ❹
Silver and gold coins ❺

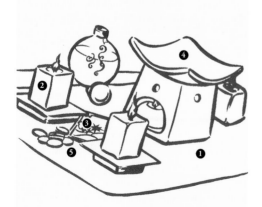

Gaze into the card, and in your imagination, see the wheel begin to spin. Look at how the spinning creates sparks that in turn generate waves of bright light. Hold your arms crossed in front of you, like an Egyptian mummy, and visualize the Wheel of Fortune spinning inside your body. Imagine that there is a new source of power being activated inside you, more powerful than anything you have ever before experienced.

Consecrate the coins by passing them through the aromatic smoke from the oil burner. Keep them safe, and in future times of stress, hold them in your hand as an amulet to provide a point of connection with the greater wealth that you have summoned forth in this spell.

This card pertains to personal power and the ability to mobilize resources in order that a particular objective may be attained. Associated with Leo, Strength is depicted overpowering a lion, representing the triumph of positive forces over negative, and spirit over matter.

STRENGTH SPELL

MAGICAL INTENTION

To release magical capabilities and realize your potential; to attain great honors, recognition, and admiration; to rise rapidly in your chosen profession; to improve self-esteem and achieve success in competition; to wipe away regrets and remorse.

MAGICAL WORKING

Dress the candles with oil and place one at each of the four compass points of the altar. Light the candles, lay the Strength card between them, and recite:

By north, south, east, and west, I summon the powers of light. Raphael of the east, appear before me! Michael of the south, appear before me! Gabriel of the west, appear before me! Uriel of the north, appear before me!

YOU WILL NEED

White altar cloth ❶
Four red candles ❷
Jasmine essential oil ❸
Strength card ❹
Parchment or paper ❺
Paintbrush and red paint ❻

Imagine that you can see the outlines of the archangels coming toward you from far away. See them approaching, until they stand around you by the altar. Gaze into the card, and picture it coming to life. Bring the image out from the card and into your abdomen. Imagine that inside your mind there are numerous switches, dials, and controls. Look for the one marked "Strength," and switch it as high as it will go. Look around inside this control room of the mind and see all the machines hum into life.

Draw an image that is symbolic of each archangel along the relevant sides of the parchment in red paint. This could be a cloud in the east for Raphael, a volcano in the south for Michael, a wave in the west for Gabriel, and a tree in the north for Uriel. In the center, draw the symbol of Leo (pictured above right). Picking up each candle in turn, put a dab between each angel's drawing and the Leo symbol. Leave this talisman on the altar for three days and nights so that it is fully charged, then keep it safe. You could perhaps frame it.

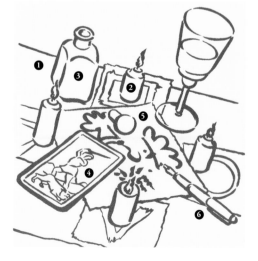

There are many references in world mythology to a man who hangs from a tree or wooden cross. In Norse legend there is Odin, who discovered the secrets of the runic letters while hanging upside down from the great world tree, Yggdrassil. Connected with Neptune, the basic meaning of this card is sacrifice; in other words, giving up one thing in exchange for something deemed of greater value.

THE HANGED MAN SPELL

YOU WILL NEED

Plain altar surface **1**
Knife **2**
Red candle **3**
Purple candle **4**
Bergamot and vetivert
essential oils **5**
The Hanged Man card **6**
Glass of water **7**

MAGICAL INTENTION

To make the wisest decision when faced with many choices; to get a new perspective; to increase stamina and the ability to make sacrifices when necessary.

MAGICAL WORKING

Inscribe your name along the side of both candles, then dress the red candle with bergamot oil and the purple candle with vetivert oil. Place the red candle in the east of the altar and the purple candle in the west, then light them. Lay the Hanged Man card in the center. Reflect back on all the times you have experienced sacrifice in your life. Think about the following themes of sacrifice:

1. Sacrificing for yourself.
2. Others sacrificing for you.
3. You sacrificing for others.
4. Others sacrificing for others.

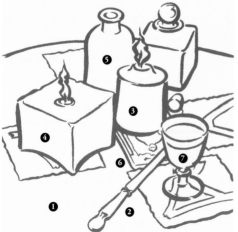

With each chain of thought, try to draw out the lessons to be learned from the experience. Now, place the red candle on top of the Hanged Man, drink all but a few drops of the water, then blow out the red candle. As you do so, visualize a spiraling band of thick, white light, almost like shining fog, rising up from the card through the candle, then encircling the altar and billowing around you. Allow yourself the sensation of being purified by this source of cosmic energy. Wherever you go, this band of power will follow you, driving away any forces that try to hold you back. When you have finished, sprinkle the remaining drops of water around the rim of the altar.

Death's job is to cut down and clear away negative conditions that have outworn their value, in order to make way for more positive influences to come in the future. Linked with Scorpio, Death represents the final illusion, and when we break through that barrier, we move into a new realm where we can function as spiritual beings, independent of time, matter, energy, and space.

DEATH SPELL

MAGICAL INTENTION

To clear away negative and unwanted influences, people, and conditions; to set yourself free from old restraints so that you can move onto new things; to send messages of love and remembrance to the departed spirits of loved ones.

YOU WILL NEED

Black altar cloth ❶
Black candle ❷
Vetivert essential oil and oil burner ❸
Death card ❹
Shallow bowl ❺
Length of black cord ❻
Scissors ❼

MAGICAL WORKING

Dress the candle with oil, place it in the center of the altar, and light it. Rest the Death card upright against the candle, and spend a few minutes gazing at the image. Pour some oil into the oil burner and light it. Pick up the oil burner (stand it in the shallow bowl if it is too hot to hold) and walk around the altar in a clockwise direction. Facing outward, salute each of the compass points by raising the burner above your head, with your arms outstretched in front of you. When you have finished, put the oil burner down on the altar, then pick up the length of cord and scissors, and cut the cord into little pieces. As you do so, recite:

Let this act of magical intention represent that, from this moment on, I have set myself free from those past influences and people with which or with whom I no longer have any real or valuable connection. In the name of the archangel Michael, so mote it be.

Direct your mind's eye to noticing just how faded and distant the recollections of those unwanted memories are. As if you were a movie director, use your camera skills to move the images farther and farther away on the horizon. Gather together the pieces of cord, and making sure no pieces are lost, place them in the bowl and burn them.

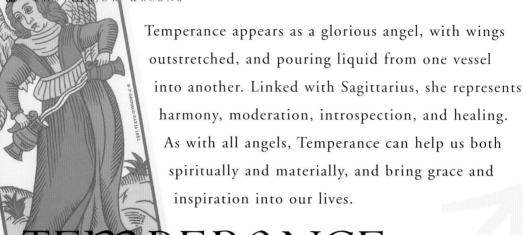

Temperance appears as a glorious angel, with wings outstretched, and pouring liquid from one vessel into another. Linked with Sagittarius, she represents harmony, moderation, introspection, and healing. As with all angels, Temperance can help us both spiritually and materially, and bring grace and inspiration into our lives.

TEMPERANCE SPELL

MAGICAL INTENTION

To bring about healing, both physically and emotionally; to help gain insight into the past so that you can understand the present more fully, and thereby influence the future.

YOU WILL NEED

Plain altar surface ❶
Gold candle ❷
Jasmine essential oil ❸
Ylang-ylang essential oil
and oil burner ❹
Temperance card ❺
Small birthday cake ❻
A few birthday cake candles ❼

MAGICAL WORKING

Dress the green candle with jasmine oil, place it in the north of the altar, and light it. Pour some ylang-ylang oil into the oil burner, place it in the west of the altar, and light it. Lay the Temperance card in the south, and put the birthday cake in the east. Moving clockwise around the altar and facing outward, salute each of the compass points by bowing. Imagine that one of the four archangels is standing at each of these points. Return to your starting point and light the candles on the cake. Placing both hands over it, ask the forces of light to bless it, reciting:

Forces of light, come to mine aid. Forces of light, come be my friend. I call upon you to listen to my request. I call upon you to assist me in attaining (specify details).

Meditate on the card, and allow it to flicker gradually into life. As you gaze into the card, imagine it growing, until you can actually step into it and talk directly to the angel yourself. Relax as much as you can. It is at this point that healing on a deep emotional and psychological level can begin to take place. When you feel that the time is right, and that you have spent enough time in this place, step out of the card. Blow out the candles on the cake, and eat some of it. Leave some of the cake as a thanksgiving to the angel, and meditate on what the angel has said to you.

Linked with Capricorn, the Devil is a symbol of negativity and destructiveness. In ancient mythology, legends tell of wars between the gods, with one side representing light and humanity, and the other evil and hatred for the human race. In this lifetime, we must each make a choice about which side we are going to pledge our allegiance to. We may try to postpone making the decision, but we cannot escape it.

THE DEVIL SPELL

MAGICAL INTENTION

To free yourself from negativity; to grant yourself forgiveness; to shut down self-destructive tendencies.

MAGICAL WORKING

Place the red candle in the west of the altar, the black candle in the south, and light them. Lay the Devil card in the north and stand the glass of wine or milk in the east. Take a couple of sips from the glass and recite:

I call upon the power of light to be with me always. Let this fortify me as I embrace the power of good over evil.

Stretch out both your hands in front of you, palms upward. On one palm, visualize yourself in miniature form, but epitomizing everything that is negative. Perhaps picture yourself with alternating expressions of envy, hatred, and fear. On the other palm, see yourself again in miniature, but radiating everything that is positive. Slowly bring both palms closer and closer to each other and toward your chest. When they touch, merge the two images of yourself together. This is now your inner self. Whereas previously there were two warring factions inside you, now there is an essential unity between the different aspects of your personality. Take another sip of wine. You have just taken an important step toward personal integration, on a very deep level.

Now visualize yourself standing on a road in two to three years' time, and looking back at this moment. Imagine some of the important events that you would like to take place after casting this spell. These events are actually waiting to happen, but need a certain amount of coaxing to bring them to the surface.

YOU WILL NEED

Plain altar surface ❶
Red candle ❷
Black candle ❸
The Devil card ❹
Glass of red wine or milk ❺

The Tower can be both a place of refuge and incarceration. Connected with Mars, it symbolizes the difficulties we all face from time to time on our spiritual journey through life, but also the cathartic quality of those difficulties, which will eventually allow us to achieve enlightenment and happiness.

THE TOWER SPELL

MAGICAL INTENTION

To establish new projects on a solid foundation; to protect financial assets; to safeguard loved ones and loving relationships; for increased health and safety; for success in martial arts and victory in battle.

MAGICAL WORKING

Dress both candles with oil, then place one in the northwest and one in the center of the altar. Light them. Lay the Tower card in the southeast of the altar, so that the candles and card run diagonally across its surface. Visualize yourself standing at the top of the battlements of an ancient tower. Over the thick walls, you can see an incredible landscape where mighty armies are on the move. You realize that you are a general, symbolically, and that the army you are directing is in fact the army of your life's forces. Moving clockwise around the altar and facing outward, summon the four archangels—Michael in the south, Gabriel in the west, Uriel in the north, and Raphael in the east—by drawing the symbol of Mars (pictured above right) in the air with the piece of iron.

Returning to your starting position, allow each of these symbols to become filled with electric light, shining like beacons in the darkness. In your mind's eye, see yourself dressed in a general's uniform, or the robes and crown of a warring king. See each of the archangels helping you prepare for the battles that lie ahead. Spend as much time as you want on this. Burn the tobacco as an offering to the spirit of battle you have just successfully invoked.

YOU WILL NEED

Red altar cloth **1**
Two red candles **2**
Cinnamon essential oil **3**
The Tower card **4**
Piece of iron **5**
Pinch of tobacco and
censer or fireproof surface **6**

XVII — THE STAR

The Star represents peace, serenity, and tranquillity. It shows us the peace we will find after having passed through life's trials, and symbolizes spiritual recuperation and repose, when we can take stock of what has passed and make plans for the future. The Star also has links with Aquarius, which represents humanitarianism and thinking of others.

THE STAR SPELL

MAGICAL INTENTION

To assist in the evolution of humanity; to render yourself worthy and able to serve others; to instigate original thought and inventiveness.

MAGICAL WORKING

Dress both purple candles with oil, then place one in the east and one in the west of the altar. Lay the Star card between the candles and light them, reciting:

In the name of the creator of all things, I open my life so that it may be filled with divine spirit. Show me the path to follow. Be with me, through my life's story, as a faithful friend and counselor. In the name of all that is good and beneficial, so mote it be.

Inscribe the symbol of Aquarius (pictured above right) in several places on the white candle, then place it on the altar above the card and light it. Draw more of the symbols at random on the altar cloth with blue chalk. Meditate on your relationship with humanity. Ask your guardian angel for advice, and let yourself be guided by it. When you feel the time is right, blow out the candles and leave some candy on the altar as a thanksgiving for your angel's advice. Repeat this ritual at the same time of day on the following two days. During that period, either when you are awake or in your dreams, you will be given a message or a vision about how your life can proceed. You may well have a flash of inspiration, or it could be something more subtle.

YOU WILL NEED

White altar cloth **1**
Two purple candles **2**
Jojoba essential oil **3**
The Star card **4**
Knife **5**
White candle **6**
Blue chalk **7**
Candy **8**

The Moon hovers high in the night sky, and can alter how we perceive things. Everything appears different at night, and it can be difficult to see the truth of what is happening. Connected with Pisces, the Moon is linked with the subconscious, and represents intuition, imagination, and sensitivity.

THE MOON SPELL

MAGICAL INTENTION

To uncover deceptions and get to the bottom of a mystery; to protect yourself against being misled; to protect you and your family against illness or psychological problems; to combat gossip and rumors; to create an attractive, mysterious presence; to attract a potential lover.

MAGICAL WORKING

Dress both candles with oil, then place one in the east and one in the west of the altar. Light them and recite:

Here I stand, invoking the presence of the Moon. Let the mists of illusion be cleared from my mind, and let me perceive the true nature of the events about which I inquire. So mote it be.

Lay the Moon card between the candles and concentrate on it. Allow it to come to life, and see yourself in it. When you are firmly inside the image, conjure the presence of your guardian angel. Let this angel take you on a journey. Be attentive to the things you are shown. The farther you travel on this journey, the more you will benefit. When the time is right, burn the fennel leaves on a fireproof surface or in a censer. When the flames have died down but smoke is still rising, place the silver coin on the bed of leaves, visualizing a silvery moon shining around you as you do so. Repeat this spell on the following two days, using all the original ingredients but new fennel leaves. When you have finished, scatter the burned leaves on the ground outside, preferably at a crossroads. Keep the coin safe, and whenever you feel the need, you can hold the coin as an amulet to reignite the Moon's astral presence. When you do so, it will give you a sense of mystery that others will recognize and find fascinating.

YOU WILL NEED

Plain altar surface **1**
Two dark blue candles **2**
Rosemary essential oil **3**
The Moon card **4**
Fennel leaves **5**
Fireproof surface or censer **6**
Silver coin **7**

The Sun represents light, health, and happiness, and symbolizes the growth and harmonious development of all aspects of life. Connected with the life-giving Sun of our own solar system, it is one of the most joyful cards of the tarot.

THE SUN SPELL

MAGICAL INTENTION

For improved health and the well-being of children; to bless the home with a fruitful year ahead; to achieve material security and an improved lifestyle; for increased travel abroad.

MAGICAL WORKING

Dress both candles with oil, then place the yellow candle in the east and the orange candle in the west of the altar. Decorate the altar with an assortment of fruit, then lay the Sun card between the candles, light them, and recite:

I hereby invoke the power of the Sun to be my friend in this lifetime. May its rays burn neither too harshly upon my face, nor too hot upon my back. May the spirits that are of the Sun be with me in all my undertakings. May success come to me, and may my life be filled with happiness and freedom. So mote it be.

YOU WILL NEED
Orange altar cloth ❶
Yellow candle ❷
Orange candle ❸
Sandalwood essential oil ❹
Assortment of fruit ❺
The Sun card ❻

Visualize a golden disk shining in the room, above your head. Let this disk slowly come down inside your head, all the way through your body. Feel the presence of the rays as they shine from within you. Let your aura become irradiated by this shining disk. Spend some time doing this. As the candles burn down, meditate on the powerful inflow of positive forces that is already beginning to make its way into your life. After you feel you have spent long enough on this, pinch or snuff out the candles; do not blow them out. Eat a portion of fruit. Repeat the spell on the following two days. When you have finished, gather up any remaining fruit and bury it at a crossroads.

Judgment is often depicted as the dead rising from their graves in the earth, about to enter into a new life. Linked with Pluto, lord of the underworld, Judgment represents powerful transforming influences, as each thing in life turns into its opposite—death into life, white into black, and so on.

JUDGMENT
SPELL

MAGICAL INTENTION

To transform your life completely; to free yourself from negative physical habits and ways of thinking; to discover new sources of material, spiritual, and emotional wealth.

MAGICAL WORKING

Dress the candles with the oil, and place them in the east and west of the altar. Light them, then lay the Judgment card in the center with the chess set and board just below. Recite:

YOU WILL NEED

Gold altar drape ❶

Two gold candles ❷

Frankincense essential oil ❸

Judgment card ❹

Chess set with board ❺

I call upon the mighty forces of the universe to come to my aid. Let these forces enable me to make the changes I want to see happening. Let the spiritual forces of this card show me where I may discover new wealth, in all its manifestations. So mote it be.

Concentrating on the card and chess set, visualize a powerful spirit army coming toward you, banners and pennants flying. As it nears, it stops, and pledges its support to you. From deep inside your mind, speak with it, and tell it what you want it to bring to you. When you have done this, send it on its way. Do not let it loiter. The temptation to sleep or break off here will be strong, but maintain control and stay awake.

Visualize the army riding off and engaging in many activities in order to bring you what you desire. Imagine a circle of vibrant, humming energy around you. You will find that you can send strands of this energy out into space, by thinking of the results that you wish to experience. Repeat this spell each day for seven days.

Depicted as a woman dancing within a circle, the World invites us to join in her joyous celebration of life. Connected with Saturn, she represents the creative processes in which we all share, the successes we have already had, and the achievements that lie ahead.

THE WORLD SPELL

MAGICAL INTENTION

To attain great honors, recognition, and material success; for blessings for your entire family; to create opportunities for trade and travel abroad; for protection when traveling and harmony in the workplace.

MAGICAL WORKING

Inscribe your name along the side of the candle. Dress the candle with oil, place it in the center of the altar, and light it. Rest the World card upright against it and recite:

YOU WILL NEED

White altar cloth ❶
Knife ❷
White candle ❸
Lavender essential oil ❹
The World card ❺
Glass of milk ❻
Bowl of fruit and grain ❼

In the name of the powerful forces of light, I call upon the elemental kingdoms to come to my aid, and bring me the success and honors that are my heart's desire. I ask also that others may benefit from the blessings that are accorded to me. In the name of the archangel Uriel, so mote it be.

Visualize Uriel standing before you. He appears in shades of green and russet, with the golden brown of the earth glinting around him. As you look at him, you can hear the rustle of leaves in the wind, and smell the odor of fresh-cut grass. Visualize a stream of gold coming from him to you. Spend as much time as you can focusing on this, and make the image as real and colorful as you can. Picture all the things you are going to do when this new prosperity reaches you. Make the imagery as vivid and physical as possible. Leave the glass of milk and bowl of fruit and grain on the altar as a thanksgiving. Repeat the spell each day for seven days. When the spellcasting is complete, bury the milk, fruit, and grain in a cemetery or at a crossroads. Within a short space of time, you will begin to see the benefits of the spell.

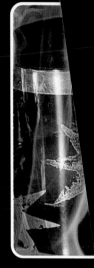

The spells in this chapter use combinations of several tarot cards from both the major and minor arcana. These are strong spells with many layers of meaning, and should be used with care. Never cast one of these spells for trivial purposes, or if you are not entirely sure you want the proposed outcome. The spells cover a wide range of situations, from fulfilling physical desires by encouraging passionate encounters, to realizing esoteric needs by granting entry into the spiritual realm of magical knowledge.

COMBINING THE CARDS

This spell uses four tarot cards: the Magician helps
you to get your message across convincingly; the High
Priestess activates your inner resources; the Wheel
of Fortune unleashes your hidden potential; and
the Star triggers inspiration of the highest order.

SPELL FOR THE ADMIRATION OF OTHERS

MAGICAL INTENTION

To enable you to shine, even in the presence of competitors; to capture the imagination
of others, and help them feel a sense of rapport with you and your objectives; to achieve
amazing good fortune.

YOU WILL NEED

White altar cloth **1**
Knife **2**
Purple candle **3**
Yellow candle **4**
Ambergris or musk
essential oil and oil burner **5**
Four tarot cards **6**
Amethyst **7**

MAGICAL WORKING

Inscribe your name along the side of both candles. Dress them with oil, then place them in
the middle of the altar and light them. Burn the remaining oil in the oil burner, positioned
in front of the candles. Lay the Magician card in the east of the altar, the High Priestess in
the south, the Wheel of Fortune in the west, and the Star in the north. Wave some of the
scented smoke from the oil burner over each of the cards, starting in the east and working
clockwise around the altar. After you have done so, recite the following three times:

*Lord Magician, Lady Priestess, bring your light to shine on me
that all may see the glory in me as I move through life. I am your
humble servant on this mortal plane. Let the immortal light of
your divine love shine within me.*

Stand by the altar, and hold the amethyst in your right hand.
Focus in your heart on the theme of love. Visualize a light
emanating from inside you, lighting up the room you are
in. Concentrate this light into a circle, and move it up above
your head. Keep focusing your thoughts on the reality of this
light. Imagine that the room is growing brighter, and when
you are ready, bring the power from this circle down into the
amethyst. Carry the amethyst with you as an amulet.

You will need seven cards for this spell: the Fool opens the gateway to new opportunities; the Knights or Queens of the four suits safeguard you on your journey; the Three of Wands sparks your powers of leadership; and the World opens the doorway to undreamed of riches.

SPELL FOR aDVENTURES IN LIFE

magical INTENTION

To enhance the sense of adventure in your life; to enable you to approach challenges or problems with zest and enthusiasm.

YOU WILL NEED

Red altar cloth **1**

Knife **2**

Three red candles **3**

Cinnamon essential oil **4**

White candle **5**

Seven tarot cards **6**

magical WORKING

Inscribe your name along the side of the red candles. Dress them with oil, place them in the north, east, and west of the altar, and light them. Inscribe the words "The world opens for me" in the white candle, continually reciting the words as you do so. Dress the candle with oil, place it in the south of the altar, and light it.

Lay the Fool card in the center of the altar. As you do so, visualize some of the experiences you have been through in your life. Lay the Queen (if you are female) or Knight (if you are male) of Coins in the southeast, the Queen or Knight of Swords in the southwest, the Queen or Knight of Wands in the northwest, and the Queen or Knight of Cups in the northeast. Consider the battles you have been through in life, and the achievements you would like to happen. Place the Three of Wands sidewise below the Fool, with the World card upright across it.

Hold your arms in the air, and imagine a vast corridor opening up in front of you, with a road stretching out, running into the distance. Behind you, four horsemen start to move forward as you step out onto the road. They are your guardians and providers as your journey opens up. It is they who will bring an abundance of opportunities, contacts, and guidance on choices that will have to be made. Imagine yourself mounted alongside them; you are now on your way.

You will need six tarot cards for this spell: the Ace of Coins represents the riches of the earth; the Four of Coins symbolizes enduring benefits; the Nine of Coins represents prestige and recognition; the World pertains to material success; the Wheel of Fortune to the theme of abundance; and the Empress to that of fertility and the seeds of possibility.

SPELL FOR THE RICHES OF

MAGICAL INTENTION
To gain the friendship of the spirits of the earth, so that they open up the gateway to great riches; to live your life in splendor.

MAGICAL WORKING
Place the oil burner containing frankincense oil in the north of the altar and light it. Lay the green cord all the way around the circumference of the altar, with the ends overlapping. Visualize a circle of golden light spinning around you and the altar to form a cone of power. Place the Ace of Coins in the north of the altar, the Four of Coins in the southeast, and the Nine of Coins in the southwest.

Hold both hands over the Ace of Coins and picture a massive doorway opening up in front of you. Let your skin feel the draft as it widens. Imagine that you can see an Aladdin's cave of treasures, stacked with ingots, sacks of silver and gold coins, and crates of precious stones. Picture yourself entering the cave and carrying some of the riches out with you. Scatter as much jewelry and money across the altar as you can.

THE EARTH

Hold your hands above the Four of Coins and visualize yourself enjoying the benefits of those riches. See yourself in your ideal home, with your perfect partner, and in a wide variety of situations. When you are satisfied, place both hands over the Nine of Coins and visualize yourself being recognized and appreciated by people. See the look of admiration and respect on their faces. Imagine the benefits that you are able to bring about in the lives of others with your new-found riches.

NINE OF COINS

Now, place the three major arcana cards on the altar in the form of a triangle. Lay the World in the south of the altar, the Wheel of Fortune in the northwest, and the Empress in the northeast. You will see that you have now constructed a six-pointed star. Imagine yourself at a future point in your life, looking back upon this moment as the starting point. Think about the planets associated with these three cards—Saturn, Jupiter, and Venus, respectively—and their spheres of influence.

Saturn represents devotion to work and completion of duties; Jupiter symbolizes abundance and hidden opportunity; and Venus governs the laws of attraction and how success may be attained through exercising charm, grace, love, and harmony.

Tie the two ends of the green cord together and place it inside the star shape you have formed. Write a list of the things you would like the universe to give you on a piece of parchment with red ink. Make them outlandish and extravagant. Place this list in an envelope, seal it, and keep it safe. Leave the altar as it is for three days, then dismantle it and untie the cord. Try to wear the cord around your waist or neck regularly over the next year. In a year's time, open the envelope; you will be surprised at how many things will have come to pass.

YOU WILL NEED

Silver silk altar cloth ❶
Frankincense essential oil and oil burner ❷
Length of green cord ❸
Six tarot cards ❹
Pieces of gold and silver jewelry ❺
Paper currency and coins ❻
Parchment or paper ❼
Pen with red ink ❽
Envelope ❾

This spell requires three cards: the Two of Wands allows you to take the lead in discussions; the Magician gives you persuasive powers; and the Star enables you to shine like a star, above all others.

SPELL FOR
INTERVIEW SUCCESS

MAGICAL INTENTION

To succeed in an interview; to acquire a radiant light around you that will win others over to your side in all kinds of stressful situations; to gain friends and influence people.

MAGICAL WORKING

Dress the candles with the oil, then place the red candle in the north of the altar and the white candle in the east. Lay the Two of Wands card in the west of the altar, and balance the Magician and Star cards upright against each other in the south. Take your time doing this, so that they do not fall over during the spellcasting. If this does happen, stand them upright once again and repeat the spell from the beginning. Light the candles and recite:

I call upon the spirit of Hermes, lord of communication, to be present with me at my interview. (Give the date, time, and place of the interview if possible.) May the spirits take note that the gods have decreed that I have been chosen as the successful candidate.

Sprinkle some salt around the perimeter of the altar, then sprinkle the remaining salt around the Magician and Star cards. While the candles burn down, focus your mind on an image of you walking out from the interview with the interviewer by your side, and going off to lunch together or for a drink. As you walk, you are both laughing and chatting, as if you have known each other all of your lives.

YOU WILL NEED

Plain altar surface **1**
Red candle **2**
White candle **3**
Frankincense essential oil **4**
Three tarot cards **5**
Salt **6**

Five cards are needed for this spell: the Wheel of Fortune contributes hope and inspiration; the Magician grants intellectual prowess; the Hermit increases analytical powers; the Three of Coins represents apprenticeship; and the Eight of Coins exemplifies

SPELL FOR   gaining mastery of a craft.

PASSING EXAMINATIONS

MAGICAL INTENTION

To pass examinations with flying colors; to succeed in competitions; to gain mastery in your chosen field of study or work.

MAGICAL WORKING

YOU WILL NEED

Plain altar surface ❶
Two purple candles ❷
Lavender essential oil ❸
Five tarot cards ❹
Piece of coral or quartz ❺
Gold and silver tinsel
or paper ❻

Dress both candles with oil, place them in the north of the altar, and light them. Lay the Wheel of Fortune card in the northwest of the altar, and the Magician in the northeast. Visualize the force of these cards beginning to spill out onto the surface of the altar, and like a liquid, down onto the floor around you. Close your eyes and feel the liquid slowly spreading around your feet. Lay the Hermit card in the southwest of the altar, and the Three of Coins in the southeast, then place the Eight of Coins in the center.

Let the energies of the cards emanate around you until you feel a spinning sensation. After some time, visualize this force becoming a smaller circle, and let it move up and down your body. When you are ready, bring this energy into your hands, and then pick up the piece of coral or quartz and let the force flow into it. Holding the stone to your chest, visualize seeing yourself collecting your certificate, or receiving the news that you have passed, and recite:

I hereby call upon my own unconscious mind to achieve its full potential so that I may pass this examination (give title and date of examination) and progress to my next stage of development.

Sprinkle gold and silver tinsel or paper all over the altar in celebration, and carry the stone with you to your examination as a powerful amulet.

You will need three tarot cards for this spell: the Chariot will send you off in top gear toward your goal; the Magician enhances your intellectual resources of memory, reason, and intelligence, and the ability to use your experience in a constructive manner; and the Hermit grants carefulness.

SPELL FOR PASSING a DRIVING TEST

MAGICAL INTENTION

To pass your driving test; to help you improve your driving skills; to give you a sense of well-being and achievement in general.

YOU WILL NEED

Gold altar cloth ❶
Red candle ❷
Yellow candle ❸
Hyssop or fennel essential oil ❹
Three tarot cards ❺
Parchment or paper ❻
Pen with red ink ❼

MAGICAL WORKING

Dress both candles with oil, place the red candle in the east of the altar and the yellow candle in the west, and light them. Lay the Chariot card in the center, with the Magician on the right and the Hermit on the left. Visualize these three forces combining to help you attain your objective. Picture yourself in a car, in complete control of everything happening inside the car, and with full knowledge of everything happening outside it.

Draw a small cartoon-style sketch on the parchment in red ink or paint showing you driving around in a car. This drawing does not have to be very ornate; matchstick-style people will do. When you have finished drawing, lay the parchment across the cards, raise both hands over it, and recite:

I hereby call upon the power of the cards to assist me in improving my driving skills. Let this moment represent the point in time when I pass my driving test. So mote it be.

Visualize all the possible mistakes you might make during your test in as much detail as you can, then picture yourself completing every aspect of the test perfectly. Run through this set of images quickly, then very slowly, then quickly again. Take the drawing with you to your test as a talisman.

Use five tarot cards for this spell: the Six of Coins establishes the principle of sharing; the King, Queen, and Page of Cups summon the men and women with whom you can explore the theme of friendship and affinity;

and the Six of Cups enhances the ability to care about others.

SPELL FOR FRIENDSHIP

MAGICAL INTENTION

To expand and develop warmth, affinity, comradeship, and unity with those living and experiencing life on similar wavelengths.

MAGICAL WORKING

Inscribe the word "Friendship" along the side of both candles. Dress them with the oil, then place one in the east and one in the west of the altar. Light both candles. Lay the tarot cards in a lucky horseshoe shape in the center of the altar in the following order: Six of Coins, King of Cups, Queen of Cups, Page of Cups, and Six of Cups. Recite:

Let these cards represent the forces of friendship in my life. May this quality be blessed in my life, and may the friendships of past, present, and future be a source of happiness and fulfillment for me. May I also be a source of blessing for those with whom I have friendship. In the name of the archangel Gabriel, so mote it be.

Meditate on past and present friends. Visualize yourself sitting in a circle of orange light, and imagine that this light is something you can send across time and space to the people

YOU WILL NEED

Green altar cloth **1**
Knife **2**
Two green candles **3**
Ylang-ylang essential oil **4**
Five tarot cards **5**

in your memory. As it reaches them, their faces light up with smiles as they are reminded of you, and they wave to you in greeting. Spend some time doing this. There is no hurry.

As you look at the cards on the table, imagine you can see interconnecting lines of energy running between them. Each card begins to flicker with movement as this energy travels from one to another. They appear to pulsate with a life force. Visualize a green ray of light emanating from the cards and surrounding you, and feel filled with the love and friendship of others. Continue this visualization for as long as you wish.

Six cards are used in this spell: the Five of Coins shows where an area of instability may lie, and reveals how you may best deal with it; the Two of Cups opens the way for new encounters; Temperance creates a spiritual dynamic through which you can absorb previous experiences and learn from them; the Ten of Cups questions the realm of commitments; the Ten of Coins adds the element of stability and material consistency; and the Lovers sets the scene for the entire theme of love and choices in matters of love.

SPELL FOR ENHANCING

MAGICAL INTENTION

To explore love on every physical and emotional level; to open yourself up to whatever the gods and goddesses of love may wish you to learn; to bring a greater flow of love and affection into your life.

MAGICAL WORKING

Dress the candles with oil, place one in the east and one in the center of the altar, and light them. Using the chalk or cord and starting in the east, draw or form a large spiral clockwise around the perimeter of the altar, gradually moving in toward the center. You will have to walk around the altar to do this. Stop about a quarter of the way into the center.

Place the Five of Coins at the point at which you have stopped the spiral. Look at the card, and picture two people together, but suffering from loneliness and misery. Although they are traveling in the same direction, each is very much alone.

L♀VE

See yourself as one of these characters, lonely and without love. Continue drawing or forming the spiral until you are about half of the way into the center. Place the Two of Cups at this point, and as you do so, recognize that this card represents your journey toward meeting someone, however circuitous the route may be. Recite:

I call upon the archangel Haniel, archangel of the sphere of Venus, to bring about a meeting with the person who is to become my soul mate, in accordance with my own greater spiritual good, and that of the other person. So mote it be.

As you recite these words, lay the Temperance card alongside the Two of Cups. Imagine that you can hear the rustle of wind or wings. Haniel appears before you; the lower two-thirds of his body is light green, the upper third pink. Spend some time in building this image. You may get the sensation of the room becoming warmer as this happens, or your body heating up. Either way, it is a good sign.

Light some incense, then continue the spiral until you are three-quarters of the way into the center of the altar. Lay the Ten of Cups and the Ten of Coins at this point, then continue the spiraling pattern into the center. Lay the Lovers card in the center. Look at how the spiral interconnects all the cards, and as you look down upon the last card, reflect on how much happiness and emotional stability you are shortly going to experience in the new loving relationship that you have brought into being.

Attach the red cord to the ring, hold it above the altar like a pendulum, and allow it to spin in a circular direction, following the course of the spiral. As it spins, recite: "Soul mate, Soul mate, Soul mate." When the ring has stopped spinning, wear it around your neck for seven days as an amulet, keeping it on even when you take a bath or shower. After this period, keep both the ring and the cord as a reminder of the spell you have cast.

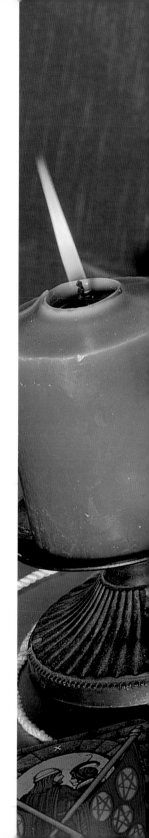

YOU WILL NEED

Gold altar cloth **1**		Six tarot cards **5**
Two green candles **2**		Musk or sandalwood incense	
Rose essential oil **3**		and censer or oil burner **6**
White chalk or length of		A ring, preferably gold **7**
white cord **4**		Length of red cord **8**

This spell uses four tarot cards: the Two of Cups represents a new loving relationship; the Page of Wands symbolizes a new person entering your life unexpectedly; the Lovers show the opportunities for love in your life; and the Eight of Wands depicts something coming into your life very quickly.

SPELL FOR PASSIONATE ENCOUNTERS

MAGICAL INTENTION

To unleash the desires of those around you; to turn your own sparks of fantasy into the flames of actual experience.

YOU WILL NEED

Red altar cloth ❶
Red candle ❷
Orange candle ❸
Rose essential oil ❹
Four tarot cards ❺
Flower petals ❻
Hourglass ❼
Selection of sensual thanksgiving offerings ❽

MAGICAL WORKING

Dress the candles in the oil, then place the red candle in the north of the altar and the orange candle in the south. Light them and recite:

I call upon the forces of love and light to bring me a passionate lover so that we can enjoy each other's company and lovemaking.

Lay the Two of Cups with the Page of Wands across it in the west of the altar, and the Lovers with the Eight of Wands across it in the east. Sprinkle some flower petals all around the altar and recite:

Let the spirits take note, for the gods have decreed that I am to be given a hot, passionate lover for my pleasure. May my joy be made full. So mote it be.

Recite three times. Place the hourglass in the center of the altar, turn it upside down, and think about the passionate encounters you would like to have until all the sand runs through. Picture yourself in vivid detail in as many different sexual situations as you like. Leave chocolates, scent, makeup, sexy clothing, or a sex toy on the altar as offerings. Repeat the casting on three days in a row. When you have finished, take all of the offerings and bury them quite deeply in a secluded place. The more lavish the thanksgiving offering, the speedier and more impressive the result.

This spell uses five tarot cards: the Lovers symbolizes the choices to be made regarding who you are going to love; the Seven of Cups represents confusion concerning love matters; the Two of Cups symbolizes a new phase in a loving relationship; the Eight of Swords represents frustration and the need to cut yourself free; and the Two of Swords symbolizes the ability to make the right choice.

SPELL FOR GETTING RID OF a LOVER

YOU WILL NEED

Plain altar surface **1**
Red candle **2**
Black candle **3**
Five tarot cards **4**
Salt **5**
Glass of water **6**
Lock of your lover's hair or a small piece of sheepskin **7**
Bowl of rose petals **8**

MAGICAL INTENTION

To free yourself from a relationship in which you feel trapped, so that both you and your lover can move onto new pastures without any feelings of hurt, betrayal, or heartbreak.

MAGICAL WORKING

Place the red candle in the north of the altar, the black candle in the south, and light them. Lay the Lovers card in the center and recite three times:

Here I place myself and (give his/her name). May the gods look down, and help me to send him/her on his/her way.

Lay the Seven of Cups card in the west of the altar, with the Two of Cups across it, and recite three times:

Here he/she is, looking the other way, his/her emotions changing, shifting, and moving away from me.

Lay down the Eight of Swords with the Two of Swords across it in the east of the altar, and recite three times:

Here he/she goes, unable to find his/her way back. He/she is gone for good now. So mote it be.

Sprinkle a little salt in each of the four compass points, then repeat with sprinkles of water. Place the lock of your unwanted lover's hair in the bowl of rose petals in the center of the altar and set them alight.

Four tarot cards are needed for this spell: the Devil represents negativity in all its forms; the Tower depicts things tumbling down; the King of Swords symbolizes victory; and the Nine of Wands represents barricades of protection.

SPELL FOR VANQUISHING TROUBLESOME PEOPLE

MAGICAL INTENTION

To break a connection with someone who has become a troublesome influence; to set yourself and the other person free, so that you can both move in different directions and get on with your lives in peace.

YOU WILL NEED

Black altar cloth ❶
Red candle ❷
Black candle ❸
Four tarot cards ❹
Pieces of broken glass or a few rusty iron nails ❺
Bottle ❻

MAGICAL WORKING

Lay the Devil card in the north of the altar and the Tower in the south. Stand the red candle on top of the Devil and the black candle on top of the Tower. Light the candles and recite:

Hail the wind, hail the storm, let peace return to my life and may (give name of the person) be sent away wherever is best for him/her to be, but not near me, for my life is grieved and burdened by his/her presence. So mote it be.

Repeat three times, each time more slowly and more powerfully. Place the broken glass or rusty nails in the bottle, repeating the name of the troublesome person for several minutes. Seal the bottle, and put it between the two candles. Place the King of Swords on top of the bottle (lay the bottle on its side if necessary) for several minutes, then pick up the card in one hand and the bottle in the other, and play-act your card fighting with the bottle, emerging victorious. Put the bottle to one side, then lay the Nine of Wands alongside the King of Swords in the center of the altar. Recite:

Let this be my moment of victory, and now that (give name) has gone, the sun will shine on me and on him/her.

This spell requires nine tarot cards: Justice brings balance to the situation; Judgment indicates that the dispute will soon be over; the King and Queen of Swords act as judges; Strength represents yourself; the Eight of Swords symbolizes your enemy; the Six of Wands evokes victory; the Four of Coins encourages financial gain; and the Six of Coins brings financial redress from your enemy.

SPELL FOR
SETTLING DISPUTES

MAGICAL INTENTION

To obtain a favorable outcome in a dispute or legal matter. It should be something important that will affect your life substantially for years to come, not just a minor problem.

MAGICAL WORKING

Place the candles in the middle of the altar, a little apart from each other, and light them. Place Justice and Judgment between and just below the candles. Salute the cards by saying aloud:

Justice, I ask you for your help to bring this dispute to a favorable outcome. Please show your mercy and wipe away any negative karma I may have brought upon this event, and give me improved understanding for the future. Judgment, I ask that you influence the forthcoming events in my favor so that your greatness may be magnified. So mote it be.

Place the King and Queen of Swords, one on either side of Justice and Judgment. Holding Strength in your right hand, and the Eight of Swords in your left, use the former to demolish the latter in a mock battle. Then place the Eight of Swords face down below Justice and Judgment to show its defeat. Place Strength face up above them, between the candles.

YOU WILL NEED

Black altar cloth **1**

Two red candles **2**

Nine tarot cards **3**

Glass of milk or brandy **4**

Chocolates **5**

To seal the victory, place the Six of Wands, Four of Coins, and Six of Coins in a row above Strength. Give thanks for your success by placing a small glass of milk or brandy and a few chocolates on the altar. Leave the altar as it is for three days, lighting the candles each day for as long as you have time. When the three days are over, bury the thanksgiving offerings at a crossroads.

Use four cards for this spell: the Sun represents the power of life; the Six of Cups adds the influence of youthfulness; the Ten of Cups symbolizes your commitment to the child; and the Empress represents the child and contributes harmony.

SPELL FOR PROTECTING CHILDREN

MAGICAL INTENTION

To protect children from harm; to fill your child's life with happiness, joy, security, gentleness, and harmony.

MAGICAL WORKING

Inscribe the name of the child (or children) along the side of both candles. If you are casting this spell for an unborn child, inscribe the word "Baby" unless you know what its name will be. Dress the candles with oil, place them in the east and west of the altar, and light them. Place the oil burner containing essential oil in the north of the altar and light it. Sit quietly for a few moments, thinking about the child and the happy times that you hope lie ahead for him or her. Visualize the altar vibrating with life, as it prepares to send an important message into the outer realms of the universe. Recite:

May the unseen forces gather themselves around this child (give name), that he/she shall be safe from any harm, physical and non-physical. I call upon all the forces of spirit to protect this child wherever his/her footsteps shall lead, now and in the future. I call upon the spirits of our ancestors to be with him/her for all time, so that kind and benevolent forces may lead him/her to pathways of happiness and fulfillment.

Recite this three times. Lay the Sun card in the north of the altar, with the Six of Cups in the southeast and the Ten of Cups in the southwest. Draw or form the shape of a triangle around the perimeter of these cards with green chalk or cord. Place the Empress in the center of the altar and draw or form three circles around it with red chalk or cord. Visualize the child(ren) for whom you are casting this spell actually inside the card, within the protective circles and triangles.

This spell requires five cards: the World denotes stability; the Nine of Coins symbolizes recognition and acknowledgment; the Ten of Coins represents organization; and the King and Queen of Swords act as guardian powers of the spirit world.

SPELL FOR PROTECTING THE HOME

MAGICAL INTENTION

To protect your home and all your loved ones; to make your home a stable, well-run environment in which all who live there can thrive; to help everyone live together in harmony and mutual respect.

MAGICAL WORKING

Inscribe the address you wish to protect along the side of both candles (the number or name of your house will do). Dress the candles with oil, place them anywhere on the altar, and light them. On the parchment, draw a picture of your home in red (it can be a very simple drawing). Draw a spiral emanating outward from the front door, going around and around the house in a clockwise direction. Put the parchment in the center of the altar and lay the World card above it. Place the Nine of Coins on the left of the World and the Ten of Coins on the right.

Meditate on the spiral emanating from your drawing, and imagine it flowing around the cards and filling the room you are in. Visualize your home, and see this spiral of powerful, active energy surrounding it. See your family members inside the home, protected by this force. Lean the King and Queen of Swords against the two candles and recite:

Let these two cards represent the guardian forces that now surround and pervade my home. Let only the influences of good enter in, and may the spiritual and angelic forces that now surround my home be active and vigilant. In the name of the archangel Gabriel, so mote it be.

Keep the drawing safe as a talisman; it would be a good idea to frame it and hang it above the inside of your front door.

YOU WILL NEED

White altar cloth **1**
Knife **2**
Two white candles **3**
Ylang-ylang essential oil **4**
Parchment or paper **5**
Pen or paintbrush with red ink or paint **6**
Five tarot cards **7**

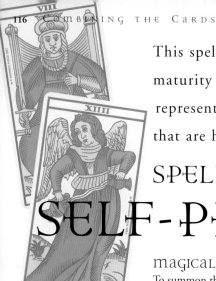

This spell combines three tarot cards: Temperance denotes maturity and harmony; the King or Queen of Swords represents the mighty warring powers of the universe that are hidden within you; and Justice symbolizes balance and a just outcome.

SPELL FOR SELF-PROTECTION

MAGICAL INTENTION

To summon the secret powers of the universe to assist in your endeavors; to receive the protection of the spirits against those who are against you.

MAGICAL WORKING

Inscribe your name along the side of both candles. Dress them with oil, place them in the east and west of the altar, and light them. Lay the Temperance card alongside the candle in the west, and the King (if you are male) or Queen (if you are female) of Swords next to the candle in the east. Take the red ribbon and make a figure-eight shape around the card and candle in the east, and the card and candle in the west. Recite:

I dedicate these candles unto my own protection so that they can light up my way. I dedicate Temperance to represent my guardian angel, and the King/Queen of Swords to represent myself, a warrior in the ways of the world.

As you do so, think about some of the troubles you have been through, and how you have survived and triumphed. Tie the two ends of the cord together, and as you do so, recognize the symbolic linking that is now taking place between you and your guardian angel. Very carefully inscribe a simple X shape on the tail side of the coin. This is the runic letter gifu, which means gift. Rub some of the essential oil into the coin, and allow it to dry. Place Justice in the center of the figure eight. Holding the coin above the card, imagine a stream of golden light traveling around the red cord, through the card, and up into the coin. Allow the sensation of warmth and power to flow through your body. Keep the coin with you as an amulet.

YOU WILL NEED

White altar cloth ❶
Knife ❷
Two red candles ❸
High John the Conqueror or jasmine essential oil ❹
Three tarot cards ❺
Length of red ribbon ❻
Metallic coin ❼

This spell requires four cards: the Emperor represents decisive action and independence; the Five of Wands imparts the power to push through obstacles; the Three of Wands teaches leadership over others; and the Seven of Wands gives the power to tackle obstacles systematically.

SPELL FOR SELF-EMPOWERMENT

MAGICAL INTENTION

To become empowered and bursting with charisma; to bring new projects to fruition; to transform brilliant ideas into real goals.

YOU WILL NEED

Red altar cloth ❶
Two red or orange candles ❷
Bergamot essential oil ❸
Four tarot cards ❹
Diamond or crystal ❺

MAGICAL WORKING

Dress both candles with oil, place them in the east and west of the altar, and light them. Place the Emperor card in the center of the altar, and put the diamond or crystal on top of it. Such stones are formed under massive pressure deep within the earth, so they represent the process by which the creation of real value takes place. Be aware of how you are like a diamond—through adversity and the pressure of opposing forces in your life, you have become a being of value.

Lay the Five, Three, and Seven of Wands in the north of the altar. Reflect on the struggles you have been through; on the battles you have won, and on those you have lost. Spend as long as you like on this. Conjure in your mind all those lost opportunities, setbacks, and scenarios of disempowerment. As they appear, imagine that they turn into a liquid, and flow down from your mind, along your spine, into your left hand. Hold your left hand over the Wand cards, and picture these images flowing into them. These cards act as a valve, allowing negativity to enter them, but letting nothing back out. Recite:

I stand here, at this point of my life, understanding why certain events have transpired the way they have. Now I am ready to move forward, may the unseen forces of good grant that I am now worthy and ready to enter this new phase of life.

Carry the diamond or crystal with you as an amulet.

This spell uses six tarot cards: the Hierophant represents knowledge and accumulated awareness; the Page of Wands shows how to apply that knowledge to your own life; and the Aces of the four suits represent the value of new beginnings.

SPELL FOR
SELF-INITIATION

MAGICAL INTENTION

To set in motion powerful forces that will allow you to move into the inner circle of spiritual and magical traditions; to achieve a flexible, receptive state of mind so that you can understand your inner self more completely.

MAGICAL WORKING

Holding the bottle of lavender oil, concentrate your thoughts around the theme of searching. At first, nothing may seem to happen; but if you continue, spiritual energies will eventually flare and spark around you. Lay the tarot cards on the altar in a random pattern. Visualize the power of your own mind walking into the cards, like a hitchhiker in the middle of the desert suddenly finding the pyramids and entering one. Now go within, deep within, until you come across a statue of black obsidian stone. What does this statue say to you? What might be its meaning? Here, more than anywhere else, you might feel that someone is trying to talk to you. Allow this state of mind to continue for as long as you desire, conversing with the spirits.

YOU WILL NEED

Blue altar cloth ❶
Lavender essential oil ❷
Six tarot cards ❸
Oak leaf ❹

Pour a few drops of oil onto the oak leaf, then walk clockwise around the altar, facing outward and holding up the oak leaf in front of you at each of the four compass points. Return to your starting position, and place the leaf in the center of the altar. Recognize that the generations of the initiated that have gone before you constitute the main trunk of the tree, and that your life is symbolized by this leaf. Bury the leaf at a crossroads or cemetery.

Use three tarot cards for this spell: Temperance helps you to learn from the past; Judgment allows you to go into new experiences with a sense of celebration; and Death represents the negative, disempowering influences of the past.

SPELL FOR UNCOVERING SECRETS

MAGICAL INTENTION

To reveal hidden secrets that are restricting you and preventing your progress; to understand the true reasons of your current situation so that you can move forward to a new phase.

MAGICAL WORKING

Inscribe your name along the side of both candles. Dress them with oil, place them in the east and west of the altar, and light them. Lay the Temperance card in the center of the altar, and lean the Judgment and the Death cards against the candles in the east and west, respectively. Recite:

In the name of the archangel Gabriel, I call upon the forces of light to uncover the secrets concerning (specify what you would like to gain enlightenment about) and to bring me a deeper understanding of the events that brought it to pass. I stand at the doorway, and humbly seek admission to the secrets and mysteries concerning this matter.

Pick up the stone and blow on it to represent consecration by air. Sprinkle it with water to symbolize consecration by water. Hold it over one of the candles to represent consecration by fire, then rub some of the salt into it to symbolize consecration by earth. Holding the stone in your hand, allow your mind's eye to scan the situation from a variety of different angles. Keep the stone with you as an amulet until you receive enlightenment.

YOU WILL NEED

Plain altar surface **1**
Knife **2**
Two blue or purple candles **3**
Dragon's blood or
clove essential oil **4**
Three tarot cards **5**
Small stone **6**
Glass of water **7**
Salt **8**

Three cards are used in this spell: the Magician helps you to learn, absorb, and organize the information inside yourself; the High Priestess assists in making intelligent, intuitive application of that information; and the Hierophant provides entry to the secret areas of the mind.

SPELL FOR GAINING MAGICAL KNOWLEDGE

MAGICAL INTENTION

To understand the causes of things, so that you can influence events in alignment with your own desires; to discover your destiny; to learn the ways of the spirit world.

YOU WILL NEED

Black altar cloth ❶
Knife ❷
Black candle ❸
White candle ❹
High John the Conqueror or vetivert essential oil ❺
Three tarot cards ❻
Mirror or crystal ball ❼

MAGICAL WORKING

Inscribe the word "Cause" along the side of the black candle and "Effect" along the white candle. Dress both candles with oil, place the black candle in the east of the altar and the white candle in the west, and light them. Lay the Magician card in the center of the altar, then lean the High Priestess upright against the white candle, and lean the Hierophant upright against the black candle.

Place the mirror or crystal ball on the altar. Gaze into it, and imagine that you can see things moving within it. Throughout your countless lifetimes, deep within the reel of data banks of your unconscious mind, there exists an enormous repository of knowledge. Imagine massive computers coming to life in your head; their screens begin to glow with multicolored flashing lights and humming sounds fill the air. Inside this imaginary control panel, look around for the dials marked "Knowledge," "Love," "Fortune," and "Good Health." Reset each of these dials to maximum. Notice how this affects the lights and sounds. Something is beginning to happen, deep inside your unconscious mind; you are triggering long-dormant psychic and magical consciousness. Recite:

In the name of the universal powers of understanding, I give thanks for all the help I have received toward my evolution, and call upon all that is evolutionary to continue working with me toward these same ends. So mote it be.

INDEX

CREDITS

Quarto would like to thank and
acknowledge the following for allowing
us to reproduce images of their tarot
cards in this book:

Illustrations from the Visconti-Sforza,
Dragon, and Morgan-Greer tarot
decks reproduced by permission of
US Games Systems, Inc, Stamford,
CT 06902, USA. Copyrights © 1975,
1996, and 1993 respectively by US
Games Systems, Inc, Stamford, CT.
Further reproduction prohibited.

Illustrations from the Tarot de Marseille
reproduced by permission of France
Cartes Grimaud, 49 rue Alexandre,
BP 49, 54132 Saint Max Cédex, France.
Further reproduction prohibited.

We would also like to thank Charlie's
Rock Shop, London, for kindly allowing
us to photograph their products.

All other illustrations are the copyright
of Quarto. While every effort has been
made to credit contributors, Quarto
would like to apologize should there
have been any omissions or errors.

Terry Donaldson is the director of
the London Tarot Training Centre and
can be contacted via its website at
www.tarottrainingcentre.com and by
email at healingwhiteray@yahoo.com.